James Thomson Callender

The Political Progress of Britain

An Impartial History of Abuses in the Government of the British Empire, in

Europe, Asia and America. Third Edition

James Thomson Callender

The Political Progress of Britain
An Impartial History of Abuses in the Government of the British Empire, in Europe, Asia and America. Third Edition

ISBN/EAN: 9783744762380

Printed in Europe, USA, Canada, Australia, Japan

Cover: Foto ©Suzi / pixelio.de

More available books at **www.hansebooks.com**

THE
POLITICAL PROGRESS

OF

BRITAIN:

OR, AN

IMPARTIAL HISTORY

OF

ABUSES IN THE GOVERNMENT

OF THE

BRITISH EMPIRE,

IN

Europe, Afia, and America.

FROM THE REVOLUTION, IN 1688, TO THE PRESENT TIME :

THE WHOLE TENDING TO PROVE THE RUINOUS CONSEQUENCES OF
THE POPULAR SYSTEM OF

TAXATION, WAR, AND CONQUEST.

" THE WORLD'S MAD BUSINESS."

PART FIRST.

Third Edition.

PHILADELPHIA:

PRINTED BY AND FOR *RICHARD FOLWELL*, No. 33, MULBERRY-STREET.

1795.

[PRICE HALF A DOLLAR.]

ADVERTISEMENT.

THE first edition of *The Political Progress of Britain* was published at Edinburgh and London, in Autumn, 1792. The sale was lively, and the prospect of future success flattering. The plan was, to give an impartial history of the abuses in government, in a series of pamphlets. But while the author was preparing for the press, a second number, along with a new edition of the first, he was, on the 2d of January, 1793, apprehended, and with some difficulty made his escape. Two booksellers, who acted as his editors, were prosecuted; and after a very arbitrary trial, they were condemned, the one to three months, and the other to six months of imprisonment. A revolution will take place in Scotland before the lapse of ten years at farthest, and most likely much sooner. The Scots nation will then certainly think itself bound, by every tie of wisdom, of gratitude, and of justice, to make reparation to these two honest men, for the tyranny which they have encountered in the cause of truth. In Britain, authors and editors of pamphlets have long conducted the van of every revolution. They compose a kind of forlorn hope on the skirts of battle; and though they may often want experience, or influence, to marshal the main body, they yet enjoy the honour and the danger of the first rank, in storming the ramparts of oppression.

The verdict of a packed jury, did not alter the opinions of those who had approved of the publication. Five times its original price hath, since its suppression, been offered in Edinburgh, for a copy. At London, a new edition was printed by Ridgway and Symonds, two booksellers, confined in Newgate, for publishing political writings. They sell the pamphlet, and others of the same tendency, openly in prison. It is next to impossible, for despotism to over-whelm the divine art of printing.

A copy of the first edition was handed to Mr. Jefferson, late American Secretary of State. He spoke of it, on different occasions, in respectful terms. He said, that it contained, " the most " astonishing concentration of abuses, that he had ever heard of " in any government." He enquired, why it was not printed in America? and said, that he, for one, would gladly become a purchaser. Other gentlemen have delivered their opinions to the same effect; and their encouragement was one cause for the appearance of this American edition. In preparing it for the press, a multiplicity of new materials presented themselves to the recollection of the writer. Hence the Introduction hath swelled to more than its former size. By indulging this habit of enlarging, as he went on, the author has found it impossible to re-print the whole of the original pamphlet, as he at first designed. When he came to examine his performance at the distance of two years, he saw many topics of importance that had been but slightly touched; and whatever related to his native country, he was anxious to make as perfect as possible. Instead, therefore, of correcting an old work, he has, in a great measure, formed a new one; but he has avoided any mention of facts, or any reference to publications, posterior to the date of the original Introduction. A mixture of this kind would have confused his narrative; because, since it was first written, the internal state of Britain hath undergone a very great alteration. The scene is varying every day; and on a subject so complicated, and, at the same time, so fluctuating, he cannot, at the distance of a thousand leagues, write and delineate with the confidence of an eye-witness. He might also, with probability, have been suspected of partiality, had he attempted to touch on a subject, wherein he was so personally interested; and where he might have forgot that decorum of stile and sentiment, which the public are entitled to demand. The history of the two last years, is, therefore, entirely passed over; and the reader is here presented with a kind of original ground-plan, of those follies and crimes of government, which laid the foundation of a British, and in particular, of a Scots insurrection. This little volume, forms a general introduction to the perusal of those trials at Edinburgh, for sedition, that have been printed, and to those others, for high treason, that will possibly be soon printed in the United States.

The work was at first intended for that class of people, who had not much time to spend in reading, and who wanted a plain, but substantial meal of political information. The facts are, therefore, crouded together as closely as possible. All the coquetry of authorship has been avoided. The ambition of the writer was to be candid, unaffected, and intelligible; because, truth is the basis of sound argument, simplicity the soul of elegance, and perspicuity the supreme touch-stone of accurate composition.

A report was circulated, and believed, in Scotland, that this production came, in reality, from the pen of one of the judges of the court of session. The charge was unjust. His lordship did not write a single page of it; but he said openly, that its contents were authentic, and unanswerable; and that the public were welcome to call it his.

For the extreme rashness of his original plan, the writer cannot offer an apology that prudence will accept. A short story may, perhaps, convey the motives of his conduct. In 1758, the duke of Marlborough, with eighteen thousand men, landed on the coast of France. The troops, when disembarking, were oppofed by a French battery, which was immediately filenced; for it confifted only of an old man, armed with two mufkets. He was flightly wounded in the leg, and made prifoner. The Englifh afked him, whether he expected, that his two mufkets were to filence the fire of their fleet ? " Gentlemen," he replied, " I " have only done my duty ; and if all my countrymen here, had " acted like me, you would not this day have landed at Cancalle."

PHILADELPHIA, *November* 14, 1794.

POSTSCRIPT.

A Third Edition of *The Political Progrefs of Britain* is now fubmitted to the public. Since the appearance of the fecond, in November laft, a pamphlet has been publifhed, entitled, *A Bone to gnaw for the Democrats,* or, *Obfervations on a pamphlet entitled, The Political Progrefs of Britain.* The author is offended at my prefumption in having predicted a Scots revolution. The multiplied diforders in the government itfelf, feem alone fufficient for putting an end to it. Two years have now elapfed, fince the war began with France. The experiment has already coft Britain at leaft fixty thoufand lives, and between the augmentation of her public debt, the capture of her merchant fhips, and the bankruptcies produced by the various calamities of war, at leaft fixty millions fterling. For the expences of a third campaign, fhe is contracting a debt of twentyfour millions fterling ; and of this fum, fix millions are to be beftowed upon Francis the fecond, that the fighting machines of Germany, may be led, or driven, to a twentieth defeat. The following paragraph in a London paper, of the 29th of April, 1793, demonftrates how incapable Britain is of fuch convulfive exertions.

" According to lord Rawdon's affecting ftatement, in his new " bill, there are no lefs than *twenty thoufand* debtors, *one thoufand* " *three hundred wives,* and *four thoufand children,* now in *confine-* " *ment.*" The number muft at prefent be fuppofed far greater.

The Public Ledger, of the 21ft of June, 1793, advances one good reafon for the alacrity of George the third, in commencing this war.

" The hundred thoufand pounds, for which a treafury war- " rant has been granted, as part of the fubfidy for the Hanoveri- " an troops, has been added to the two millions, feven hundred " thoufand pounds, already placed in the funds, in the name of " the lords of the regency of Hanover."

This is a minifterial newfpaper. Thus we learn, that this amiable monarch fells the lives of *one* part of his fubjects, for the money of another. In the present tempest of political disquisition, it is not possible that such a system as the British constitution can long hold itself together.

The church is, if possible, more corrupted than the state. " An old woman, last year, was confined about six months, in " the king's bench prison, and paid above *one hundred pounds* " *costs*, for refusing to pay church fees to the amount of *two* " *shillings and eight-pence.*"*

The first campaign against France, was to cost about twelve millions sterling to Britain, and the third requires twenty-four millions. By the same rule, the fifth campaign should cost forty-eight. The regal and ecclesiastical plunder of the late French government, and the estates of seventy-thousand emigrants, have been computed at about three hundred and eighty-five millions sterling of property in the hands of the republic. If to these, we add the revenues of Austrian Flanders, and other conquered countries, with the acquisition of perhaps six millions of subjects, we shall soon be convinced, that Britain, supported only by credit, can have but a poor chance in contending with the inexhaustible resources of her antagonist. The contest may be protracted for three or four campaigns, but it can hardly fail to end in the destruction of the British monarchy.

JAMES THOMSON CALLENDER.

Philadelphia, 3d of March, 1795.

---

* Morning Chronicle, 6th May, 1793.

CONTENTS.

INTRODUCTION.

Of British wars since the revolution—Immense slaughter—Expence of wars—Nootka Sound—Oczakow—Tippoo Saib—Amount of national debt—Enormous extent of its interest in the next century—Scandalous **terms** *on which it was* **first** *contracted—Sketch of the civil list of* **William III.**—*Profligate expenditure of the court—Hints for royal economy—Queen Anne—A single default of thirty-five millions sterling—Lotteries—Earl of Chatham—Specimen of British taxes—Lord North—His extravagant premiums for money—Scheme of paying off public debt—Its futility—Uniform absurdity of modern British* **wars**—**Impress of Seamen**—**Character and design of** *this work.* PAGE 9

CHAP. I.

Purity *and importance of Scots representatives in parliament—Parchment barons—Anecdotes of the Scots excise—Window tax—Extracts from an authentic report to the lords of* **the treasury**—*Herring fishery—Salt and coal duties—Dreadful oppression—Fate of Sir John Fenwick—History of the creditors of Charles the second—Summary of the public services of the prince* **of** *Wales.* 28

CHAP. II.

Fertility of the Hebrides—Islay—Its prodigious improvement—Immense abundance of fish—Miserable effects **of excise**—**Salt and coal duties**—*Specimen of Scots sinecures.* 47

CHAP. III.

Reports of the commissioners of public accounts—Crown lands—Astonishing corn law—British famine in the reign of William third—Striking picture of Scotch wretchedness at that period—What Scotland might have been—War in **general**—*Culloden—The bloody Duke.* 63

C H A P IV.

Blackstone—His idea *of the English constitution—Default of an hundred and seventy-one millions sterling—Powell—Bembridge—Mary Talbot—Westminster election—Anecdotes of the war with America—English Dissenters—Their lawsuit with the corporation of London—Society of friends—Unparalleled oppression of that sect in England—Boxing.* 82

C H A P. V.

*Civil list—Accumulation of fifteen millions—*Dog kennels*—George the first—His liberal ideas of government—George the second—His hospitality at the burial of his eldest son—Excise.* 97

C H A P. VI.

*Edward I.—Edward III.—Henry V.—Ireland—Conduct of Britain in various quarters of the world—Otaheite—Guinea—North-America—The Jersey prison-ship—Bengal—*General *estimate of destruction in the East-Indies.* 109

INTRODUCTION.

Of British wars since the Revolution—Immense slaughter—Expence of wars —Nootka Sound—Oczakow—Tippoo Saib—Amount of National debt—Enormous extent of its interest in the next century—Scandalous terms on which it was first contracted—Sketch of the civil list of William III.—Profligate expenditure of the court—Hints for royal economy—Queen Anne—A single default of thirty-five millions sterling—Lotteries—Earl of Chatham—Specimen of British taxes—Lord North—His extravagant premiums for money—Scheme of paying off public debt—Its futility—Uniform absurdity of modern British wars—Impress of Seamen—Character and design of this work.

SINCE the year one thousand six hundred and eighty-eight, Britain has been once at war with Holland, five times at war with France, and six times at war with Spain. The expulsion, or flight of James the Second, produced a bloody civil contest both in Scotland and Ireland. Since that time, we have also been disturbed with two rebellions in Britain, besides an endless catalogue of massacres in Asia and America. In Europe, the price which we advance for a war, hath successively extended from one hundred thousand lives, to thrice that number; and from thirty to an hundred and thirty-nine millions sterling. From Africa we import annually between thirty and forty thousand slaves, an estimate which rises, in the course of a century, to at least three millions of murders. In Bengal only, we destroyed or expelled, within the short period of six years, five millions of industrious and innocent people* ; we have been sovereigns of high rank, in that country, for about thirty-five years† ; and there is reason to compute, that, since our elevation, we have strewed the plains of Hindostan with thirty-six millions of carcases‡. Combining the diversified ravages of famine, pestilence, and the sword, it may justly be supposed, that in these transactions, fifteen hundred thousand of our countrymen have perished; a number equal to that part of the whole inhabitants of Britain who are at present able to bear arms. The destruction of our French and Spanish antagonists, and of German, Sardinian, and Portuguese mercenaries, purchased by Britain to fight against them, has amounted to at least a second fifteen hundred thousand lives. Hence it follows, that British

---

* Dow's History of Hindostan, quarto edition, vol. iii. page 70.
† On the 23d of June, 1757, Colonel Clive defeated Suraja Dowla, Nabob of Bengal. This victory laid the foundation of the territorial grandeur of the East-India Company.
‡ Infra. Chap. vi.

B

quarrels, in only an hundred years, have deprived Europe of three millions of men, in the flower of life, whose defcendants, in the progrefs of domeftic fociety, muft have expanded into multitudes beyond calculation. The perfons deftroyed, have in whole, certainly exceeded thirty millions, that is to fay, three hundred thoufand acts of homicide *per annum*. Thefe victims have been facrificed to the balance of power, and the balance of trade, the honour of the Britifh flag, the rights of the Britifh crown, the " *omnipotence* of Parliament*," and the fecurity of the Proteftant fucceffion. Proceeding at this rate for another century, we may, with that felf-complacency, which is natural to mankind, admire ourfelves and our atchievements ; but every other nation in the world muft be entitled to wifh, that an earthquake or a volcano, fhould firft bury the whole Britifh iflands together in the centre of the globe ; that a fingle, but decifive exertion of Almighty vengeance, fhould terminate the progrefs and the remembrance of our crimes.

In the fcale of juft calculation, the moft valuable commodity, next to human blood, is money. Having made a grofs eftimate of the wafte of the former, let us endeavour to compute the confumption of the latter. The expences of Britifh wars, from the revolution to the end of the year 1789, has been ftated, by Sir John Sinclair, at three hundred and feventy-feven millions, twenty-nine thoufand five hundred and ninety-eight pounds fterling. The particulars are as follows, viz.

Expences of war, during the reign of William III. - - - - -	£.30,447,382
Queen Anne, - - - - - -	43,360,003
George I. - - - - - -	6,048,267
Expence of the war begun anno 1739, -	46,418,689
Ditto of the war begun anno 1756, - -	111,271,996
Ditto of the American war, - -	139,171,876
Ditto of the armament refpecting Holland, in 1787, - - - - -	311,385
Total,	†£.377,029,598

Since this publication, a fleet has been armed againft Spain, to enforce the privilege of killing whales at the fouth pole, and wild cats at twice that diftance. By the account of the minifter himfelf, as laid before parliament, the affair coft us three millions one hundred and thirty-three thoufand pounds‡. In point of economy, this project refembled the commencement of a lawfuit in chancery to recover half a crown. We have fince quarrel-

---

* This modeft phrafe was current before the American revolution. It hath, fince that time, been laid afide.

† Hiftory of the public revenue of the Britifh empire, part iii. chap. 2d.

‡ New Annual Regifter, for 1791. page 141.

led with Catharine of Ruffia, for a few acres in the defarts of
Tartary; and the charges of this fecond armament muft alfo
have been very confiderable. Thirty-three fhips of the line, and
about thirty thoufand men, were kept up for four months, that
the grand Turk might recover poffeffion of Oczakow, and after
all, this notable fcheme was difappointed. At prefent, we are
tearing afunder the dominions of Tippoo Saib ; and Mr. Fox
lately faid, in the houfe of commons, that this war, which has
juft now been ended, went on at an expence to ourfelves of two
hun ired and fifty thoufand pounds fterling per month, or about
eight thoufand guineas per day. Comprehending thefe frefh exploits, the amount of money deburfed from the exchequer, on
account of war, fince the revolution, muft exceed three
hundred and eighty millions fterling. We are alfo to fubjoin the
value of fixteen or twenty thoufand merchant-fhips, taken by
the enemy. This diminutive article of fixty or an hundred millions fterling, would have been fufficient for tranfporting and
fettling eight or twelve hundred thoufand farmers, with their
wives and children, on the banks of the Sufquehannah or the
Miffiffippi. So numerous a colony of cuftomers could well have
been fpared from the nations of Europe. They would foon have
rivalled the population of France, and have required a greater
quantity of manufactures than this ifland has ever prepared for
exportation. Inftead of fo comfortable a profpect, we are, as a
nation, indebted to the extent of at leaft two hundred and fifty
millions. The annual intereft of this fum, the neceffary expences
of management, and of collecting the revenue that defrays it,
are, all together, above *eleven millions and an half fterling*. This
burden is equivalent to a yearly poll-tax of one pound three
fhillings fterling, per head, upon every individual inhabitant of
Britain*. Befides what we pay at prefent upon this account, it
is worth while to notice what we have paid already. From the
revolution to the year 1789, inclufive, the intereft of the public

* In an affair of fo much importance, the utmoft accuracy may be expected.
The exact amount of the debt, as ftated by Sir John Sinclair, is *two hundred and
forty-feven millions, nine hundred and eighty-one thoufand, nine hundred and twenty-feven pounds,
five fhilling, and ten-pence.* Hiftory of the public revenue, Part III. ch. p. v. In
another place, near the end of the fame chapter, he has thefe words. " Thus, in-
" cluding the finking fund, and the intereft of our unliquidated claims, our
" public debts, at prefent, require the fum of *ten millions, fix hundred and thirty-two
" thoufand, one hundred and ninety-one pounds fourteen fhillings, and three half-pence per
" annum.*" The expence of collecting this fum, in proportion to that of the whole
Britifh revenue, may be gueffed at about nine hundred thoufand pounds a year,
which, added to the intereft itfelf, gives the eleven millions and an half, ftated
in the text. The preface to the volume here quoted, bears date the 30th of
January 1790. The Spanifh and Ruffian fquabbles muft, between them, have
coft at leaft fix millions fterling. They took place after the preceding eftimate had
been made of the extent of the national debt ; fo that the fums mentioned in the
text are, both as to the principal and the annual charges, much about the fact,
even after deducting what Mr. Pitt may have paid off.

debts, and of the public loans repaid, including other incidental articles connected with thefe matters, has been three hundred and ninety millions, two hundred and feventy-fix thoufand,
five hundred and feventy-nine pounds*.

But this is a trifle compared with the fums of intereft that we
muft difcharge in the next hundred years. The burden hath now
rifen to eleven millions, and five hundred thoufand pounds fterling *per annum*. Six yearly payments only, from the 1ft of January,
1792, to the 1ft of January 1798, inclufive, with compound intereft at five per cent. from the firft of thefe two dates to the
fecond, amount to eighty millions, nine hundred and fifty-four
thoufand, three hundred and forty feven pounds, four fhillings
and three-pence. The reader may profecute the feries of figures
to the end of the next century. He will then difcover that feveral myriads of millions fterling are not for that time alone, equal
to the preffure of this enormous load. We far excel the Greeks
and Romans in the arts of induftry, and the refources of wealth;
but it would be vain to fearch among ancient nations, for any inftance that rivals Britifh debts, and Britifh folly.

It is an object of the higheft curiofity and importance for every
one of us, to enquire, in what manner fuch aftonifhing fums have
been borrowed, and by what methods they have been expended?
In the courfe of this work, each of thefe queries will be explained; but in the mean time, a few detached particulars fhall be
here inferted, to affift the reader in forming a conception of the
reft of the bufinefs.

In the war of 1689, that feed-bed of the future calamities of
Britain, money was borrowed upon annuities for lives. " Four-
" teen *per cent.* was granted for one life, twelve *per cent.* for two
" lives, and ten *per cent.* for three. Such terms were, *in the high-*
" *eft degree extravagant;* particularly as no attention was paid
" to *difference of ages*†."

The fame author adds, on the authority of Dr. Price, that
" borrowing, at the rate of twelve *per cent.* for two lives, and
" ten *per cent.* for three, is giving ten *per cent.* for money
" in the one cafe, and nine *per cent.* in the other‡." From 1690,
to the end of the war, the hiftorian fays, that, on the money
borrowed, " eight *per cent.* was uniformly paid." To raife a farther fum upon thefe annuities, another expedient was, in the fequel, embraced. The annuitants were offered a reverfionary intereft, after the failure of their lives, for *ninety-fix years*, to be reckoned
from January 1695, on their paying only four and a half year's
purchafe, or fixty-three pounds for every annuity of fourteen
pounds. In 1698, the demand was reduced to four years pur-

* Hiftory of the public revenue, &c. Part III. chap. 2d.
† Ibid. Part II. chap. 4.   ‡ Ibid.

chafe; or fifty-fix pounds for the annuity of fourteen. For our
farther fatisfaction, " the fame fyftem was afterwards adopted
" in the reign of Queen Anne*." Some of thefe annuities remain, at this day, " to the amount of one hundred and thirty-
" one thoufand two hundred and three pounds, feven fhillings,
" and eight-pence *per annum* for which the fum of one mil-
" lion eight hundred and thirty-fix thoufand, two hundred and
" feventy-five pounds, feventeen fhillings and ten pence three
" farthings, had been originally contributed; and for the ufe
" of which, the public muft pay above *thirteen millions* before
" they are all extinct†."

But even all this was only a part of the evil. " Davenant
" affirms, that the debt of the nation was fwelled more by *high*
" *premiums* than even by the exorbitant intereft that was paid;
" and that its credit was at fo low an ebb, that *five millions*, giv-
" en by parliament, produced for the fervice of the war, and
" to the ufes of the public, but little more than *two millions and*
" *an half‡*" In another paffage, he feems to contradict himfelf,
and to reduce the loffes in this way to *one* million out of five;
but there is full evidence on record, that his firft computation
was more accurate than the fecond.

" In 1698, a propofal was made to parliament, of advancing
" two millions to government, at eight per cent. provided the
" fubfcribers were erected into a new Eaft-India company, with
" exclufive privileges. The old Eaft-India company offered fe-
" ven hundred thoufand pounds, nearly the amount of their
" capital, at *four* per cent. upon the fame conditions. But fuch
" was, at that time, *the ftate of public credit*, that it was more
" convenient for government to borrow two millions at *eight*
" per cent. than feven hundred thoufand pounds at *four*. The
" propofal of the new fubfcribers was accepted‖." The two millions coft an intereft of one hundred and fixty thoufand pounds.
The feven hundred thoufand pounds could have been had at
four per cent. that is, for twenty-eight thoufand. Out of the
two millions, therefore, feven hundred thoufand pounds were
only worth twenty-eight thoufand pounds, and the remaining
one hundred and thirty-two thoufand of intereft, was the fum
really paid for the remaining thirteen hundred thoufand pounds
of principal. Thus, the latter fum, in fact, coft the public ten
per cent. with an overplus, on the whole, of two thoufand
pounds. Thefe details are perhaps dry, but they are fufficiently
intelligible, and all men of fenfe will acknowledge, that they
are extremely ufeful. If British hiftorians had uniformly com-

* Hiftory of the public revenue, &c. Part ii. chap. 4.   † Ibid.
‡ Ibid.
‖ Inquiry into the nature and caufes of the Wealth of Nations, Book V.
Chap. I. Part 3d, Article I.

posed their works on this plan, we should long since have re-
nounced entirely, or, at least, in a great degree, the practice of foreign wars. With all proper deference to Quintilian, such a
stile is preferable to that of any historical writer in his long
catalogue of literary heroes. Let us return, with these useful cal-
culations, to the reign of William.

The management of this money, when obtained, corresponded with the terms of the loan. In the reign of William the
Third, the civil list, that *cup of abominations*, was supported by
certain taxes, appropriated for that purpose, and which amounted " at an average, to about six hundred and eighty thousand
" pounds *per annum*[*]." The public revenue of England, after
every possible extortion, was only screwed up to three millions,
eight hundred and ninety-five thousand, two hundred and five
pounds[†]; so that the civil list was less than one-fifth, but more
than one-sixth part of *the whole revenues of England*. If the civil
list of this day bore the same proportion to the national income,
it would extend to at least *three millions sterling*. Sir John Sinclair
has given a complete state of the whole expences of the civil
list, during the thirteen years of the reign of the Protestant hero.
A few articles may serve as a specimen of the rest. To the robes,
fifty-seven thousand pounds. This money would have clothed two
thousand poor people, at forty shillings each, *per annum*, for thirteen years, with a reversion of five thousand pounds for the dress
of the royal family, which consisted, properly speaking, but of
two persons. Jewels *sixty thousand pounds*. Plate, *one hundred and
two thousand pounds*. Band of gentlemen pensioners, *sixty-nine
thousand pounds*. To making gardens, besides an account paid under a different head, *one hundred and thirty-three thousand pounds*.
After setting apart thirty-three thousand pounds for his gardens,
William could have applied the rest of this money much better. He might have parcelled out of the crown lands, which
are to this day lying waste, in the centre of England, two thousand small farms. On each of his tenants, he might have bestowed fifty pounds to begin the world ; and the first ten years
of a perpetual lease, free of rent. To the stables, *two hundred
and thirty-five thousand pounds*. To the great wardrobe, *three
hundred and nineteen thousand pounds*. This sum would have
clothed an army of sixty thousand men ; or, what is more esti-
mable, ten thousand tradesmen and their families. Privy purse,
four hundred and eighty-three thousand pounds. For half this money,
we might have had a beautiful edition of all the Greek and Roman classics, with English translations. To the treasurer of the
chambers, *four hundred and eighty-four thousand pounds*. This
sum would have been of the utmost service, in paving and light-

[*] History of the public revenue, Part III. chap. I.   [†] Ibid.

ing the streets of London. To the treasurer of the late Queen,
whose sister, Queen Anne, William did not think worth a plate-
full of green peas*, *five hundred and six thousand pounds*. To
the prince and princess of Denmark, a harmless but useless
couple, *six hundred and thirty-eight thousand pounds*. Fifty-three
thousand debtors, at twelve pounds each, might have been relieved from prison by this money ; or a fund might have been established with it, for the annual discharge of a thousand prisoners of that kind, on the birth-day of his majesty, and an
equal number on the day, when he signed a warrant for the mas-
sacre of Glenco. Secret services, *seven hundred and seventy-five
thousand pounds*. Fees and salaries, *eight hundred and fifty-eight
thousand pounds*. Pensions and annuities, *six hundred and eighty-
six thousand pounds*. Cofferer of the household, *thirteen hundred
thousand pounds*. In the end of the last century one shilling went
farther than three can go now ; so that this sum was equal in
reality to four millions at this day. The deliverer of England,
therefore, spent what corresponds to three hundred thousand
pounds *per annum,* on his household, for thirteen years, while,
during a considerable part of his reign, his subjects, by thousands and ten thousands, expired of hunger†. To the paymaster of the works, *four hundred and seventy-four thousand pounds*.
The whole bill extends to eight millions eight hundred and eighty thousand pounds ; and it does not appear that one-fourth part
of it was expended for wise and useful purposes‡. This was the
frugality of government, at a time, when they were compelled to
borrow money, at ten, *per cent.*

In the next reign, the system was not much improved. An
English house of commons informed Queen Anne, that " there
" remained at Christmas, 1710, thirty-five millions, three hun-
" dred and two thousand, one hundred and seven pounds of
" public money unaccounted for§." In 1714, one million, eight
hundred and seventy-six thousand pounds were raised by a lot-
tery. Out of this sum, *four hundred and seventy-six thousand
pounds* were distributed among the proprietors of the fortunate
tickets. This was a premium of about thirty-four *per cent.* on
the sum actually received‖. In 1744, the charter of the East-
India company was prolonged from 1766 to 1780. This was
an anticipation of twenty-three years. The value of the
compensation, granted by the company to government, did not
exceed thirty thousand pounds¶. This was like Esau selling his
birth-right for a mess of portage. If the bargain had been de-

---

* Anecdotes of the Duchess of Marlborough.   † Infra. chap. 3.
‡ Sixteen hundred and seventy pounds for the widows of officers, appear,
like Falstaff's half-penny worth of bread, in a corner of one article.
§ History of the public revenue, Part ii. chap 4.
‖ Ibid.   ¶ Ibid.

ferred till the expiration of the former monopoly, perhaps forty times that fum could have been obtained.

Sir John Sinclair gives a " general view of PREMIUMS upon
" the new loans," in the war of 1756.* Thefe premiums amount
in value to *fourteen millions, two hundred and eighty-three thoufand, nine hundred and feventy-five pounds fterling*. The total fum
borrowed, and added to the national debt, for this premium,
was feventy-two millions, one hundred and eleven thoufand,
and four pounds. The premium is, within a perfect trifle, *one-
fifth part* of the whole money obtained. Thus, out of every
twenty fhillings of the loan, we gave back four fhillings as a
reward for the lender. At this rate, the Britifh armies conquered Guadaloupe and Canada ; and we continue to boaft of the
glory of thefe exploits. Yet a perfon might, with as much reafon, burn his houfe, for the fake of roafting an egg in its afhes.
We may fuppofe, that the reft of the national debt was created
upon terms at leaft equally hard ; and the fifth part of the
whole two hundred and fifty millions contracted, gives a premium of FIFTY MILLIONS STERLING. After fuch work, it is
not wonderful, that we are now harneffed in debts and taxes,
like horfes in a carriage. One-third part of the expences of a
family confift in the payment of public burdens. Five hundred thoufand people in England are fupported by charity.†
We muft give twenty-fix pounds fterling *per annum* for leave
to keep a hackney coach ; and twenty fhillings *per annum* for
leave to make a farthing candle, befides one penny *per* pound
of excife upon the manufacture ; nine-pence per pound of importation duty for Peruvian bark ; and three guineas for leave to
fhoot a partridge worth two-pence. Half the price of a bottle
of wine, or a bowl of punch, goes off in taxes, for leave to
drink it. This deferves not to be termed the language of ma-
lignity. Thofe who pay the reckoning have a right to read the
bill.

> I am no orator as Brutus is,
> To ftir men's blood ; I only fpeak right on.
> I tell you that which *you yourfelves do know*.

---

* Part II. chap. 4.

† Dr. Wendeborn, a candid, and well informed writer, in his View of England, towards the clofe of the eighteenth century, fays, that " whoever lives
" upon a thoufand a year, is fuppofed to pay at prefent about *fix hundred* of it
" in government duties, taxes, excife, church parifh and poor rates."

He alfo obferves, that of the people of England, " *one million* is fo poor it
" muft be fupported by the reft." Thefe affertions have been confiderably
foftened in the text, to avoid any charge of exaggeration. They do not apply
to Scotland, where beggars are lefs numerous, and parifh and poor rates but
little known.

As a neceffary confequence of this enormous taxation, the author informs
us, that " fifty years ago, a family might live very handfomely on five hundred
" pounds *per annum*, but a thoufand will at prefent *hardly go fo far*."

On the 27th of December, 1791, a bill for an additional duty on malt, came before the house of peers. On this occasion, lord Kinnoul said, that " their lordships were not perhaps apprised " of the rate at which *barley*, in its various forms, was already " taxed; if they were not, the enumeration would astonish " them. As malt only, it was taxed at the rate of ten shillings " and six pence per quarter. The additional duty of three " pence per bushel would raise it to twelve shillings and six " pence per quarter. When to this were added the land tax, " and the duties on beer, which he severally calculated, it " would be found, that the raw commodity, which brought " the proprietor of the soil on which it was raised, about *nine* " *shillings*, paid to government, in its several stages, above *two* " *pounds ten shillings*†." Every person who advanced a part of these two pounds ten shillings, would make a separate charge on his customer for the advance of his money, so that these two pounds ten shillings would finally cost the drinker of the liquor at least three pounds ten shillings, perhaps four or five pounds; and all this on an article originally worth nine shillings. The calculation of four or five pounds, being charged for two pounds ten shillings, will not seem unreasonable, if we consider what follows. A tax of a penny per bottle, or some such trifle, was once imposed by lord North on the retailers of wine. To the surprise of all men, the vintners of London instantly raised the liquor six pence per bottle. If Britain pays at present eighteen millions sterling of taxes to the crown, we may fairly compute that she pays at least twelve millions of an additional, though invisible tax, to the landholders, merchants, and manufacturers, who, in the first place, advance the money. At the opening of a ministerial budget, there is never heard any notice as to this silent but most inevitable and terrible of all taxes. Between this burden, and that of tide-waiters and excise-men, it may be feared, that every shilling which goes into the exchequer, has, upon a medium, cost two shillings to the nation.

One other instance only shall be subjoined in this place, of the manner in which public debts have been contracted. In 1781, Lord North received for the national service twelve millions sterling. For this sum he gave eighteen millions of *three per cent.* stock, and three millions of four *per cent.* stock. The annual interest of these two sums is six hundred and sixty thousand pounds, or five and an half *per cent.* for the twelve millions actually received. Money is not commonly advanced in England, at more than four and an half *per cent.* of interest; and very frequently at four *per cent.* At the former of these two rates, the twelve millions borrowed by Lord North ought

† *Senator,* Vol. I. page 245.

only to have coft five hundred and forty thoufand pounds per
annum. The *one hundred and twenty thoufand pounds* additional, at twenty-five years purchafe, make a premium of *three
millions fterling* for the loan of *twelve millions.* It is not fur-
prifing that Sir John Sinclair, Dr. Swift and other writers,
complain fo loudly of the fcandalous conditions upon which the
public debts of Britain have been borrowed. The original contractors with government for lending of the money, remind us
of a band of ufurers, embracing every advantage over the ne-
ceffities of the ftate ; while the minifters of the crown feem
like defperate gamefters, who care not by what future expence
they fecure another caft of the dice. From the facts above
ftated, the public funds prove to be a ftupendous mafs of fraud,
profligacy, impofture and extortion. Behold that facred edi-
fice of *national faith*, that political *fanctum fanctorum*, which
we fupport at an annual expence of eleven millions and an half
fterling !*

What kind of gentry fome of thefe creditors are, there was
no body better able to inform us than the late Earl of Chatham.
" There is a fet of men," fays he, " in the city of London,
" who are known to live in riot and luxury, upon the plunder
" of the ignorant, the innocent, and the helplefs, upon that
" part of the community, which ftands moft in need of, and
" beft deferves the care and protection of the legiflature. To
" me, my Lords, whether they be miferable jobbers of Change-
" Alley, or the lofty Afiatic plunderers of Leadenhall Street,
" they are all equally deteftable. I care but little whether a man
" walks on foot, or is drawn by eight horfes, or fix horfes ;
" if his luxury be fupported by the plunder of his country, I
" defpife and abhor him. My Lords, while I had the honour
" of ferving his Majefty. *I never ventured to look at* THE TREA-
" SURY, *but from a diftance* ; it is a bufinefs I am unfit for,
" and to which I never could have fubmitted. The little I
" know of it, has not ferved to raife my opinion of what is
" vulgarly called the *monied intereft.* I mean that BLOOD-SUCK-
" ER, that MUCKWORM, which calls itfelf the friend of Go-
" vernment, which pretends to ferve this or that adminiftration,
" and may be purchafed on the fame terms *by any adminiftra-
" tion.* Under this defcription, I include the whole race of
" commiffioners, jobbers, contractors, clothiers, and remit-
" ters†."

---

* Of the original commencement of this debt, the characters, motives, and emolu-
ments of its authors, the reader may find an authentic hiftory in the *Political Progrefs*,
Part II. which will appear in a few months.

† *Vide* his fpeech in the debate on Falkland's Iflands, which has been re-printed in
the Anecdotes of his Life juft publifhed. This quarrel ended, like others, in our dif-
appointment, and perhaps difgrace. Befides much expence and trouble to individuals,
the nation fquandered between three and four millions fterling.

The friends of Mr. William Pitt boaft much of the nine millions of debt, which, in a period of fix years, he is faid to have difcharged. The fcheme is an abfolute bubble. He began to buy up *three per cents*, in April 1786; at which time they fold for feventy. They rofe, almoft inftantly, to feventy-feven, and upwards. They have fince been much higher; and if the minifter fhall make any fubftantial progrefs in his plan, they will very foon reach an hundred *per cent.* and very likely go higher. Thus, as Sir John Sinclair obferves, " the more we pay, *the more we fhall be indebted*; every fhil- " ling that is laid out in purchafing ftock, *raifes the price pro-* " *portionably.*" So peculiar is the nature of this national debt, and fo very hazardous an attempt to difcharge it! To make this quite plain, it may be obferved, that when Mr. Pitt firft began to buy up ftock, the market price of the whole three *per cent.* funds, was all together but one hundred and feventeen millions, fix hundred and forty-three thoufand pounds. In two years and an half, he had purchafed a fmall part of it; but the prodigious parade that he made about this operation, raifed the price of *the remaining ftock* to one hundred and twenty-two millions, four hundred and twenty thoufand pound. The fequel, in October 1788, was, that the minifter had expended or funk *two millions and feven hundred thoufand pounds*, and yet, he left matters WORSE THAN HE FOUND THEM by *four millions, feven hundred and feventy-feven thoufand pounds*. The following ftatement puts the matter in a fhort, and clear view :

In October, 1788, the value of the whole *remaining* three per cent. ftock was   -   -   £122,420,401

Mr. Pitt, at an expence of two millions, feven hundred thoufand pounds, had before purchafed ftock to the amount of   -   -   - £2,626,000

In April 1786, before he began to buy up at all, the whole three per cents. were only at feventy per cent. or   -   -   -   117,643,308

ACTUAL INCREASE OF NATIONAL DEBT, over and above the two millions, feven hundred thoufand pounds, caft away in the purchafe of ftock   -   -   -   -   -   004,777,093

It muft be acknowledged, in favour of Mr. Pitt, that while he has augmented the principal fum of the national debt, he has reduced the annual payment of intereft. The three millions and fix hundred thoufand pounds of three *per cents.* which are paid off, coft, formerly, one hundred and eight thoufand pounds *per annum* of intereft, which is now extinguifhed. This is the fole advantage arifing to the public from the tranf-action. But there was a fhorter way to have come at this fame purpofe. Mr. Pitt and his parliament ought to have ftruck

from the civil lift a number of ufelefs penfioners, fuch, for example, as the groom of the ftole, the mafter of the horfe, the
mafter of the robes, the mafter of the hawks, twelve lords and
twelve grooms of the bed-chamber, twenty-four preachers in
his majefty's chapel at Whitehall, and the *wet nurfes* of the
prince of Wales and the duke of York*. Inftead of abolifh-
ing ufelefs places, to difcharge this annuity, Mr. Pitt fqueezed
out of the people two millions and feven hundred thoufand
pounds, which, with the expence of collecting it, comes to at
leaft three millions fterling. The extinction of a burden of
one hundred and eight thoufand pounds *per annum* has thus coft
more than it is worth. At four and an half *per cent.* three millions produce one hundred and thirty-five thoufand pounds *per
annum*; which is itfelf twenty-feven thoufand pounds more than
the annuity extinguifhed. Here we muft obferve, that ten *per
cent.* is but a moderate and ordinary profit on the capital of ftock,
either in hufbandry, commerce, or manufactures. Hence, if
thefe three millions had been fuffered to remain in the hands
of the people of Britain, they would have afforded to the community at large, at leaft three hundred thoufand pounds *per annum* of additional wealth; and perhaps twice or thrice that
fum. The flighteft and moft neceffary taxes, are, therefore,
in their own nature, very deftructive. When a tobacconift, or
a tanner, pays thirty pounds of excife, he does not merely lofe
thirty fhillings *per annum*, as the legal intereft of his money;
but he is likewife prevented from the chance of converting this
capital of thirty pounds into an augmented fum of thirty-three,
thirty-fix, or forty pounds. If the tradefman can fhove the
tax upon his cuftomers, by raifing the price of his commodities, it comes exactly to the fame point at laft, as *their* active
capitals are always, and with mathematical certainty, reduced
in an equal proportion. Thus it is evident, that every fum
raifed from the public as an impoft, or excife, muft in reality
coft them ten *per cent.* This, by the way, demonftrates the
rafhnefs of wars undertaken in defence of *a foreign trade*, fince
the fums levied to fupport the ftruggle are, every farthing of
them, drawn from the circulation of domeftic commerce; a
commerce always more fafe, and very commonly more profitable, than that which kings are fo frequently fighting for. A
commercial war is truly *cafting our bread upon the waters, that
we may find it after many days.* Now, as every million of
pounds, raifed by government from the people of Britain, is,
upon an average, at leaft equal to an annuity for ever, of an
hundred thoufand pounds, out of the pockets of thofe who pay

* In the court and city calendar, for 1775, eight of thefe ladies are charged to the
nation, at falaries each of two hundred pounds *per annum*; befides dry nurfes, work-
women, rockers, and other luggage of the fame fort.

it, the inference is, that if Mr. Pitt had underſtood or regarded the intereſt of this country, he never would have undertaken
to diſcharge a debt bearing three *per cent.* at an expence of ten ;
or, as before obſerved, an annuity of one hundred and eight
thouſand pounds, by paving a capital of three millions, pro-
ducing a yearly profit of three hundred thouſand pounds to the
holders of it. In this way Mr. Pitt pays off the public debt.
Since October 1788, ſtocks have riſen prodigiouſly ; ſo that the period here choſen for the examination of this celebrated project, is
by far the moſt favourable that can be taken. A full account
of its ſubſequent hiſtory will be given hereafter. Mr. Pitt
might as well propoſe to empty the Baltic with a tobacco pipe.
But let us admit the caſe, that he at preſent had an hundred
millions in the exchequer. The diſcharge of the public debt
is, on his principles, abſurd and unjuſt. Stocks would inſtant-
ly riſe to at leaſt an hundred ; and he begins perhaps by paying off the twenty-one millions of three and four *per cents.* for
which Lord North actually received but *twelve millions.* Thus,
after giving, as above ſtated, five and an half *per cent.* for a
loan of twelve millions, we diſcharge that original twelve millions itſelf, with *twenty-one millions.* The preſent ſcheme for
extinguiſhing the public debt is therefore impracticable, if it
were honeſt, and, as an act of robbery againſt ourſelves, it
would be diſhoneſt, if it were practicable.

But, ſuppoſing that Mr. Pitt had in reality paid off nine millions of debt, and leſſened the public burdens of its intereſt,
yet, for the ſake of an impartial and ſatisfactory argument, his
advocates ought to arrange, in an oppoſite column, a liſt of the
additional taxes which he has impoſed, and of the thouſands of
families, whom ſuch taxes have ruined.* A third column
ſhould contain a liſt of the millions which this miniſter has
waſted upon Spaniſh and Ruſſian armaments, on the unprovoked
and piratical war againſt Tipoo Saib, on the Chineſe embaſſy,
the ſucceſſive elections for Weſtminſter, the creditors of the
prince of Wales, and the nabob of Arcot, and the Baratrian
ſettlement of Botany Bay. The pretended plan of diſcharging
the national debt, on which Mr. Pitt ſometimes expatiates to
parliament, for two hours together, was but a ſorry trap for popularity ; and if " the *ſwiniſh* multitude" had been much wiſer

* In 1723, the tax on hawkers and pedlars in England, produced, in the groſs, ten
thouſand, ſeven hundred and ſeventy-three pounds ; and eight thouſand, ſix hundred
and four pounds of net income. Thus, one-fifth of the revenue was ſunk in the collection. In 1785, Mr. Pitt, cutting the ſecond inch out of a man's noſe, doubled the
tax ; and, in 1788, the total amount of it had ſhrunk to *five thouſand, four hundred
and ſixty one pounds.* Of this ſum, the net produce was but *two thouſand, one hundred and ſeventy pounds ;* three-fifths of the produce of the tax, were thus ſunk in
collecting t. This diabolical impoſt was laid for the profeſſed purpoſe of extirpating
pedlars. Crowds of them were reduced to a ſtate of ſtarving. The new addition
to the tax hath ſince been repealed. Vid. ſome account of it in the hiſtory of the
public revenue. Part III. chap. 3.

than the reft of their family, they muft, in a moment, have feen through and defpifed the artifice. The debts of Britain never will be paid ; they never can be paid ; and in the prefent way of difcharging them, they never, in juftice, ought to be paid. The hardinefs of the father of this delufion, exceeds any thing that was ever heard of ; becaufe his arguments and affumptions are, as above explained, in a ftate of hoftility with the multiplication table ; and becaufe, though religious impoftors have pretended to work miracles, yet none even of them has ever afferted that two and two make five. But though thefe debts will never be extinguifhed by the attempts of the minifter, they have certainly paffed the meridian of their exiftence. Had the war with America lafted for two years longer, Britain would not, at this day, have owed a fhilling ; and if we fhall perfift in rufhing into carnage, with our wonted contempt of all feeling and reflection, it muft ftill be expected, that, according to the practice of other nations, a fponge or a bonfire will finifh the game of funding.

What advantage has refulted to Britain from fuch inceffant fcenes of prodigality and of bloodfhed ? In the wars of 1689, and 1702, this country was but an hobby-horfe for the emperor and the Dutch. The rebellion in 1715, was excited by the defpotic infolence of the whigs. George the Firft purchafed Bremen and Verden, from the King of Denmark, to whom they did not belong. This pitiful and dirty bargain produced the Spanifh war of 1718, and a fquadron difpatched for fix different years to the Baltic. Such exertions coft us an hundred times more than thefe quagmire duchies are worth, even to an elector of Hanover ; a diftinction which, on this bufinefs, becomes neceffary, for as to Britain, it was never pretended, that we could gain a farthing by fuch an acquifition[*]. In 1727, the nation forced the fame George into a war with Spain, which ended as ufual with much mifchief on both fides. The Spanifh war of the people in 1739, and the Auftrian fubfidy war of the crown, which commenced in 1741, were abfurd in their principles, and ruinous in their confequences. At fea, we met with nothing but hard blows. On the continent, we began by hiring the queen of Hungary to fight her own battles againft the king of Pruffia, and ten years after that war had ended, we hired the king of Pruffia, with fix hundred and feventy one thoufand pounds *per annum*, to fight his own battles againft her. If this be not folly, what are we to call it ? As to the quarrel of 1756, " It was remark- " ed by all Europe," fays Frederick, " that in her difpute " with France, *every wrong ftep was on the fide of England*."

[*] The folitary muttering of Poftlethwaite, in his dictionary, is not worth naming as an exception.

By seven years of fighting, and an additional debt of seventy-two millions sterling, we secured Canada ; but had Wolfe and his army been driven from the heights of Abraham, our grandsons might have come too early to hear of an American revolution. As to this event, the circumstances are almost too shocking for reflection. At that time an English woman had discovered a pretended remedy for the canine madness, and Frederick advises a French correspondent *to recommend this medicine to the use of the parliament of England, as they must certainly have been bitten by a mad dog.*

In the quarrels of the continent we should concern ourselves but little ; for in a defensive war, we may safely defy all the nations of Europe. When the whole civilized world was embodied under the banners of Rome, the most distinguished of her conquerors, at the head of thirty thousand veterans[*], disembarked for a second time on the coast of Britain. The face of the country was covered with a forest, and the solitary tribes were divided upon the old question *Who shall be king ?* The Island could hardly have attained to a twentieth part of its present population, yet by his own account, the invader found a retreat prudent, or perhaps necessary. South Britain was afterwards subjected, but this acquisition was the talk of more than thirty years. Every village was bought with the blood of the legions. We may confide in the moderation of a Roman historian, when he is to describe the disasters of his countrymen. In a single revolt, seventy thousand of the usurpers were extirpated ; and fifty, or, as others relate, seventy thousand soldiers perished in the course of a Caledonian campaign. Do the masters of modern Europe understand the art of war better than Severus, and Agricola, and Julius Cæsar ? Is any combination of human power to be compared with the talents and resources of the Roman empire ? If the naked Scots of the first century, resisted and vanquished the conquerors of the species, what ought we to fear from any antagonist of this day ? On six months warning Britain could muster ten or twelve hundred thousand militia. Yet, while the despots of Germany were fighting about a suburb, the nation has submitted to tremble for its existence, and the blossoms of domestic happiness have been blasted by crimps, and subsidies, and press-gangs, and excise acts. Our political and commerical systems are evidently nonsense. We possess within this single island, every production both of art and nature, which is necessary for the most comfortable enjoyment of life ; yet for the sake of tea, and sugar, and tobacco, and

---

[*] Cæsar says that he had with him five legions, and two thousand Cavalry, which with the light troops, can hardly have been less than the number specified in the text. A legion, at that time, contained five thousand infantry.

a few other defpicable luxuries, we have rufhed into an abyfs
of taxes and of blood. The boafted extent of our trade, and
the quarrels and public debts which attend it, have augmented
the fcarcity of bread, and even of grafs, at leaft three hundred *per cent.*

There is no law more juft, fays Virgil, *than that the projec-
tor of death fhould perifh by his own ftratagem.* We have
fuffered in a full proportion to what we have inflicted. As to
the flaughter of our countrymen in time of war, George
Chalmers, Efq. digefts it in a ftyle perfectly fuitable to the
underftanding and the confcience of a modern ftatefman. The
Britifh ariftocracy confider the reft of the nation, as a commodity bought and fold ; and if we required abfolute evidence of
this truth, here is a full atteftation. "It is not eafy," fays
" Mr Chalmers, " to calculate the numbers who die in the
" camp, or the battle, more than would perifh from *want*, or
" from *vice* in the hamlet or city. *It is fome confola'ion*, that
" the induftrious are too wealthy and independent to covet the
" pittance of the foldier, or to court the dangers of the failor ;
" and though *the forfaken lover*, or *the reftlefs vagrant*, may
" have looked for refuge in the army or the fleet, it may admit
" of fome doubt how far the giving proper employment to both,
" (viz. that of committing robbery and murder, and of getting
" themfelves knocked on the head for it,) may not have freed
" their parifhes from *difquietude*, and from *burdens*. It is the
" *expences* more than the *flaughter* of modern war which
" debilita'e every community."[*] This paragraph explains the
memorable epithet which has been beftowed on the Britifh
nation. For if the foldiers and failors of the Britifh army and
navy had been transformed by the wand of Circe into hogs, or
even rats, it is impoffible that this writer could have fpoken
with greater indifference of their extirpation. He confiders it
as a neceffary circumftance, that a great part of the common
people muft perifh from want or from vice, unlefs they are
difcharged in the form of armies on the reft of the world.
The remedy is a thoufand times worfe than the difeafe ; and it
would be more humane to give a premium to poor people for
ftifling their infants in the cradle. "If I am a coward," fays
Jather, " who made me fo ?" What but the miferable con-
ftruction of our government can have produced fuch a horrid
neceffity ? When ten millions and an half fterling *per annum*
are due, and muft be paid to the creditors of the nation,
befides a million to the officers who collect it, when two
millions fterling are beftowed on the church of England, and
a much larger fum on penfioners of all kinds, it is impoffible,
that we fhould not find in the oppofite fcale, a correfpondent

[*] Comparative Eftimate, p. 140.

balance of want and wretchedneſs. When you raiſe up one
end of a beam above its level, the other end muſt ſink in proportion. When you give ſix or eight hundred thouſand pounds
per annum to a ſingle family, and its trumpery of a houſehold, you reduce, with mathematical certainty, thirty or forty
thouſand families to poverty. It is not difficult to ſee that
ſuch a political progreſs muſt end in a political exploſion. Mr.
Hume, after adverting to the extremely frivolous object, as he
calls it, of the war in 1756, makes this reflection. " Our
" late deluſions have much exceeded any thing known in hiſto-
" ry, not excepting even the cruſades. For I ſuppoſe there is
" no demonſtration ſo clear, that the Holy Land was *not* the
" road to paradiſe, as there is, that the endleſs increaſe of na-
" tional debts, is the direct road to NATIONAL RUIN. But having
" now *completely reached that goal*, it is needleſs at preſent to
" look back on the paſt. It will be found in the preſent
" year (1776,) that all the revenues of this iſland, north of Trent,
" and weſt of Reading, are mortgaged and anticipated forever."
He concludes with this remark : " So egregious, indeed,
" has been our folly, that we have even loſt *all title to com-*
" *paſſion* in the numerous calamities that are awaiting us."*
It is hard to ſay what Mr. Chalmers can have deſigned by
introducing, in the quotation above cited, *the forſaken lover*.
His alluſion calls to our remembrance the practice of impreſs-
ing ſeamen, and, in a work of this nature, that ſubject
deſerves illuſtration. " The power of impreſſing ſeamen,"
ſays Blackſtone, " for the ſea ſervice, by the king's commiſſion,
" has been a matter of ſome diſpute, and ſubmitted to with
" great reluctance ; though it hath very *clearly* and *learnedly*
" been ſhewn, by Sir Michael Forſter, that the practice of
" impreſſing, and granting powers to the admiralty for that
" purpoſe, is of *very antient date*, and hath been uniformly
" continued by *a regular ſeries of precedents* to the preſent time ;
" whence he concludes it to be part of the common law. The
" difficulty ariſes from hence, that no ſtatute has expreſsly de-
" clared this power to be in the crown, though many of them
" *very ſtrongly imply it†*." The crime of man-ſtealing is
much greater than that of robbery, and only juſt leſs than that
of murder, in which it has frequently terminated. A thouſand Britiſh ſtatutes, in defence of it, could not have altered
the eſſence of the guilt. When the late Spaniſh and Ruſſian
armaments were laid aſide, perſons who had been impreſſed,
were ſometimes diſcharged, at the diſtance of three or four
hundred miles from their places of reſidence, and with a bounty
of ten or fifteen ſhillings each. During the wiſe diſpute about

* Hiſtory of England, Vol. Vth. p. 475. London octavo edition, 1778.
† Commentaries on the laws of England, Book 1, Chap. 13.

D

Falkland's Islands, which were, in value to this country, below the power of figures, a workman in London was returning one evening to his family with his weekly wages. He was apprehended by a prefs-gang, and caft into the hold of a tender. His landlord, and fome other creditors, heard of what they called his elopement. They feized on his furniture, and his wife and child were turned to the door. Within a few days after, the mother was delivered of a fecond child, in a garret. When weaknefs permitted her to rife, fhe left her two naked children, and wandered into the ftreets, as a common beggar. Inftead of obtaining affiftance, fhe was reproached as an abandoned vagabond. In defpair, fhe went into a fhop, and attempted to carry off a fmall piece of linnen. She was feized, tried, and condemned to be hanged. In her defence, the woman faid, that fhe had lived reputably and happy, till a prefs-gang robbed her of her hufband, and in him, of all means to fupport herfelf and her family ; and that in attempting to clothe her new-born infant, fhe perhaps did wrong, as fhe did not, at that time, know what fhe did. The parifh officers, and other witneffes, bore teftimony to the truth of her averment, but all to no purpofe. She was ordered for Tyburn. Though her milk, if fhe had any, muft have been fermented into poifon, it feems that nobody condefcended to feek a nurfe for her child. *The hangman dragged her fucking infant from her breaft, when he ftraitened the cord about her neck.* On the 13th of May, 1777, Sir William Meredith mentioned this affaffination in the Houfe of Commons. " Never," faid he, " was there a " fouler murder committed againft the law, than that of this " woman by the law." Thefe were the fruits of what Englifhmen call *their ineftimable privilege of a trial by jury.* It would not be difficult to fill a large volume with decifions of this ftamp, though there has not, perhaps, occurred any fingle cafe which was, in all its circumftances, fo abfolutely infernal.

In this introduction, we have feen a fketch of the hiftory of certain monarchs and minifters, fome of whom re, at this day, held up as the political faviours of Britain. The reader may compare the wanton flaughter of multitudes, and the profligate expenditure of millions, with the *guilt*, as it was termed, of Mary Jones. He will then judge which of the two parties beft deferved a halter*. This little narrative may ferve as a fupplement to the very clear and learned demonftration of Sir Michael Fofter.

This publication confifts not of fluent declamation, but of curious authenticated and important facts, with a few fhort obfervations interfperfed, which feemed neceffary to explain

* The particulars of this ftory are extracted from a letter to Charles Jenkinfon, Efq. fecretary at war, by Mr. John Clark, tranflator of the Caledonian fords. The letter was printed at Edinburgh, in 1780.

them. The reader will meet with no mournful periods to the
memory of *annual* or *triennial* parliaments; for while one
haif of the members are nominated by the houfe of peers,
it is of fmall concern whether they hold their places for
life, or but for a fingle day. Some of our projectors are of
opinion, that to fhorten the duration of parliament, would be
an ample remedy for all our grievances. The advantages of
a popular election have likewife been much extolled. Yet an
acquaintance with Thucydides, or Plutarch, or Guicciardini,
or Machiavel, may tend to calm the raptures of a republican
apoftle. The plan of univerfal fuffrages has been loudly
recommended by the duke of Richmond; and, on the 16th of
May 1782, that nobleman, feconded by Mr. Horne Tooke,
and Mr. Pitt, was fitting in a tavern, compofing advertife-
ments of reformation for the newfpapers. The times are
changed; but had his plan been adopted, it is poffible that
we fhould, at this day, have looked back, with regret, on the
humiliating, yet tranquil defpotifm of a Scots, or a Cornifh
borough.

The ftyle of this work is concife and plain; and it is hoped
that it will be found fufficiently refpectful to all parties. The
queftion to be decided is, are we to proceed with the war fyftem?
Are we, in the progrefs of the nineteenth century, to embrace
five thoufand frefh taxes, to fquander a fecord five hundred
millions fterling, and to extirpate thirty millions of people?

EDINBURGH, 14th September, 1792.

THE
POLITICAL PROGRESS
OF
BRITAIN.

CHAP. I.

Purity and importance of Scots representatives in parliament—Parchment barons—Anecdotes of the Scots excise—Window tax—Extracts from an authentic report to the lords of the treasury—Herring fishery—Salt and coal duties—Dreadful oppression—Fate of Sir John Fenwick—History of the creditors of Charles the Second—Summary of the public services of the prince of Wales.

THE people of Scotland are, on all occasions, foolish enough to interest themselves in the good or bad fortune of an English prime minister. Lord North once possessed this frivolous veneration, which hath since been transferred to Mr. William Pitt; and the Scots, in general, have long been remarked, as the most submissive and contented subjects of the British crown It is hard to say what obligations have excited that universal and superlative ardour of loyalty, for which, till very lately, we have been so strikingly distinguished. Mr. Brinsley Sheridan observed, some time ago, in the house of commons, that *the Scots nation hath just as much interest in the government of Britain, as the miners of Siberia have in the government of Russia.* The assertion was at once the most humiliating and well founded. A public revenue of eleven hundred thousand pounds annually is extracted from North-Britain. Of this sum, at least six hundred thousand pounds* are lodged in the exchequer of England, a country that has incessantly, and not very decently, reproached us for poverty. It is strange

---

* History of the public revenue, Part III. chap. 6. The statement fills four quarto pages: it appears to be candid, and as authentic and accurate, as the nature of the materials would admit. Some years ago, Sir John Sinclair transmitted a letter on this subject to a society in Scotland; and I have heard Scotsmen, so sunk in the mire of Hanoverian superstition, so degraded below *the beasts that perish*, as to censure him for presumption in doing so.

that sixteen hundred thousand people should submit to pay eleven hundred thousand pounds *per annum* to a government, in the direction of which they have nothing to say. It is very natural that a nation, absorbing six hundred thousand pounds a year of our money, should be a great deal richer than ourselves; and, at the same time, it is likewise very natural, that they should despise the Scots as a people, the most abject and contemptible of the species.

To England we were, for many centuries, a hostile, and we are still considered by them as a foreign, and in effect a conquered nation. It is true, that an extremely diminutive part of us are suffered to elect almost every twelfth member in the British house of commons; but these representatives have no title to vote, or act in a separate body. Every statute proceeds upon the majority of the voices of the whole compound assembly. What, therefore, can forty-five persons accomplish, when opposed to five hundred and thirteen? They feel the absolute insignificance of their situation, and behave accordingly. An equal number of elbow chairs, placed, once for all, on the ministerial benches, would be less expensive to government, and just about as manageable. These, and every ministerial tool of the same kind, may be called expensive, because those who are obliged to *buy*, must be understood to *sell*,* and those who range themselves under the banners of opposition, can only be considered, as having rated their voices too high for a purchaser in the parliamentary auction.

There is a fashionable phrase, *the politics of the county*, which I can never hear pronounced without a glow of indignation. Compared with such *politics*, even pimping is respectable. Our supreme court have indeed interposed, though very feebly, to extirpate what in Scotland are called *parchment barons*, and have thus prevented a crowd of unhappy wretches from plunging into an abyss of perjury. But, in other respects, their decision is of no consequence, since it most certainly cannot be of the smallest concern to this country, who are our electors, and representatives; or, indeed, whether we are represented at all. Our members, with some very singular exceptions, are

* A *worthy* representative was requested by his constituents, to attend to their interest in parliament. " Damn you, and your instructions too," said he, " I have BOUGHT you, and I will SELL you." *Political Disquisitions.* vol. I. p. 280.

About twenty years ago. Sir Lawrence Dundas wrote a letter to one of his agents in the Scots boroughs, and enjoined him. at the approaching election for parliament, *not to be outbidden.* This epistle was intercepted by his opponents, and, if I mistake not, printed in the news-papers. Sometime ago, a person resided at Dumfries, who subsisted on a salary of about fifty pounds. He was a fictitious voter, and received this annuity for perjuring himself once in every seven years. His situation was a common jest, while the people in general had no more idea of the meanness of *their* political condition, than an equal number of horses in a stable. Every Scotsman may, without effort, recollect an hundred anecdotes of the same nature.

the mere fatellites of the minifter of the day ; and forward to
ferve his moft oppreffive and criminal purpofes.

It feems to have been long a maxim with the monopolizing di-
rectors of our fouthern mafters, to extirpate, as quickly as poffible, every manufacture in this country, that interferes with
their own. Has any body forgot the fcandalous breach of national faith, by which the Scottifh diftilleries have been brought
to the verge of deftruction ? Has not the manufacture of ftarch
alfo been driven, by every engine of judicial torture, to the
laft pang of its exiftence ? Have not the manufacturers of paper, printed calicoes, malt liquors, and glafs, been harraffed
by the moft vexatious methods of exacting the revenue ? Methods equivalent to an addition of ten, or fometimes an hundred *per cent.* of the duty payable. Let us look around this
infulted country, and fay, on what manufacture, except the
linen, taxation has not faftened its bloody fangs ?

In the excife annals of Scotland, that year which expired on
the 5th of July, 1790, produced, for the duties on foap, *fixty-
five thoufand pounds.* On the 5th of July, 1791, the annual
amount of thefe duties was only *forty-five thoufand pounds ;*
and by the fame hopeful progrefs, in three years more at far-
theft, our minifters will enjoy the pleafure of extirpating a
branch of trade, once flourifhing and extenfive. Two men
were, fome years ago, executed at Edinburgh, for robbing the
excife-office of twenty-feven pounds ; but offenders may be
named, who ten thoufand times better deferve punifhment.
Oppreffive ftatutes, and a moft tyrannical method of enforcing
them, have thus, in a fingle year, deprived the revenue of
twenty thoufand pounds, in one branch only, and have compelled many induftrious families to feek refuge in England ;
and then our legiflators, to borrow the honeft language of
George Rous, Efq. " have the infolence to call this GOVERN-
" MENT."

By an oriental monopoly, we have obtained the *unexampled
privilege* of buying a pound of the fame tea, for fix or eight
fhillings, with which other nations would eagerly fupply us at
half that price*. Nay, we have to thank our prefent illuftrious minifter, that this vegetable has been reduced from a rate
ftill more extravagant. His popularity began by the commutation act. Wonders were promifed, wonders were expected,
and wonders have happened ! A nation, confifting of men who
call themfelves *enligh'ened*, have confented to build up their
windows, that they might enjoy the permiffion of fipping in
the dark a cup of tea, ten *per cent.* cheaper than formerly ;
though ftill at double its intrinfic price.

* In Philadelphia, tea is cheaper by one half than in Edinburgh. At Gottenburgh
alfo, the difference, in favour of the Swedes, is very great.

Such are the glorious confequences of our ftupid veneration for a minifter, and our abfurd fubmiffion to his capricious dictates!

General affertions, unfupported by proper evidence, deferve but little attention. I fhall therefore lay before the reader fome extracts from a book publifhed in 1786, by Dr. James Anderfon. This work is hardly known, yet every friend to the profperity of Scotland ought to be intimately acquainted with its contents.

In 1785, this gentleman was employed, by the lords of the treafury, to make a tour among the Hebrides and weftern coafts of Scotland, for the purpofe of afcertaining the beft methods to promote the fifheries, and the confequent improvement of that part of the country. This commiffion, Dr. Anderfon executed, with that ardor and fidelity of invefligation, for which he has long been diftinguifhed. It is impoffible, in a fhort performance of this nature, to give an analyfis of the volume; but the following particulars will ferve to fhew, that the weftern coafts and the weftern iflands of Scotland, groan under the moft enormous oppreffion. Dr. Anderfon has printed part of a report, dated the 14th of July 1785, and made by a committee of the Houfe of Commons. They give an account of the cuftom-houfe duties collected for ten fucceffive years, in nine counties of Scotland, viz. Argyle, Invernefs, Sutherland, Caithnefs, Orkney, Shetland, Cromarty, Nairn and Moray. The expence of collection, for thefe ten years, from the 1ft of January 1775, to the 31ft of December 1784, was

	£ 51,677 13 8 3-4
The grofs produce - -	50,717 2 1 1-4
Payments exceed the produce by	942 11 7 1-2*

The committee add, that " they have little reafon to expect " a more favourable refult from their enquiries refpecting the " excife than the cuftoms." The author fubjoins, that an account of the excife had fince been publifhed, and *confirmed the truth of this obfervation.* But this is not the worft; for there is likewife to be added a part of the expence of cruifers employed under the board of cuftoms in Scotland. On an average of five years, preceding the year 1785, this charge amounted to nine thoufand eight hundred and feventy-five pounds, twelve fhillings and four-pence. " If," fays Dr. Anderfon, " we fuppofe that one half of the above expence fhould " be ftated to the account of the nine counties above mentioned,

---

* Introduction, page 63. There is an error of the prefs in fubtracting the one fum from the other, which has been here corrected.

" which *I conceive to be an under proportion*, then the expence
" on this head would be four thousand, nine hundred and
" thirty seven pounds, sixteen shillings and two-pence."*
This article is very near equal to the whole annual produce of
the customs of these nine counties. If we take the different
sums in round numbers, we may say, that the gross produce of
the customs is five thousand pounds, the expence of collecting
them five thousand pounds, and the expence of cruisers, to
prevent smuggling, five thousand pounds. Thus, in the course
of ten years, government collected fifty thousand pounds, by
disbursing one hundred thousand. There certainly never was
such a shameful system of robbery heard of, even in the annals
of the Turks, the Spaniards, or the British East-India company. Were the whole mass of British taxes collected at such
an expence, the government itself, would, in six months, become
bankrupt ; and maids of honour, and grooms of the bedcham-
ber, and the whole cloud of sinecure vermin, would vanish, like
the exhalations of a quagmire, in the tempest of revolutionary
vengeance. " A fact of this nature, when thus fairly brought to
" light, cannot fail to strike every thinking person with some
" degree of astonishment and horror. A croud of reflections
" here press upon the mind. Why are these persons oppressed
" with taxes, when the state is no ways benefitted by them ?
" Why are the other members of the community loaded with
" burthens, to enforce the payment of these unproductive taxes
" here ? From what cause does it happen that these people
" complain of taxes, while they pay next to nothing ?"† This
may be called the insanity of despotism. I shall now state,
from the same work, a few examples of the way in which this
revenue is collected.

" A man in Skye, who had got a load of *bonded* salt, used
" the whole in curing fish, save *five* bushels only, but before
" he could recover his bond, he found himself obliged to hire
" a boat and send these five bushels to Oban, which cost him
" upwards of *five* pounds expences."‡

" One would imagine, that if a man *paid the duty for his*
" *salt*, he might afterwards do with it what he pleased ; but
" this I find is not the case. Last season (1784,) a vessel was
" fitted out in haste, at Aberdeen, to catch herrings, that were
" then on the coasts. But as the owners of that vessel had no
" duty-free salt, they were obliged to purchase salt that had
" already *paid the duty*, but before they were allowed to carry
" one ounce of this salt to sea, they were further obliged *to*
" *give bond for it*, in the same form as if it had been duty-free
" salt."‖

* Introduction, page 65.　　　　　　‡Report p. 40.
† Ibid p. 65.　　　　　　　　　　　‖ Ibid p. 41.

" Again, in the year 1783, Mr. James M'Donald, in Por-
" tree, in Skye, purchased from Leith, a quantity of salt, which
" had paid duty, and shipped it by permit on board a vessel for
" Portree. It was regularly landed, and a custom-house cer-
" tificate returned for the same. With this salt he intended to
" cure fish, when he could catch them in those seas; but not
" having found an opportunity of using it in the year 1784, he
" fitted out, at his own expence, this season (1785,) a small
" sloop, to prosecute the fisheries. On board that sloop, he
" put some part of this salt with the permit along with it.
" A revenue cutter fell in with his vessel, and *seized vessel and
" salt, provisions and all together!"*

There is an excise duty upon foreign salt, imported into the
Western Islands, of ten shillings *per* bushel, besides a custom-
house tax of about two pence three farthings.† The excise duty
is too high to be paid for salt employed in the curing of fish.
Government, therefore, in order to encourage the British fisheries, has promised to remit the excise duty. But it is possible
that the salt thus disburdened of the ten shillings of excise, might
be applied to some other purpose than that of curing fish, and
in this way, the intended bounty might be converted into a
source of fraud against the excise revenue. When the legislature,
therefore, granted this indulgence, " all importers of foreign
" salt were required first to land it at a custom-house, where it
" was to be carefully weighed by the proper officers, and the
" importer either to pay the duty, or to enter it *for the purpose*
" *of curing fish*, and in that case, to give bond, with two suffi-
" cient sureties, either to pay the excise duty of ten shillings
" *per* bushel, or *to account for the salt*, under a penalty of twenty
" shillings *per* bushel. In consequence of this bond, he must
" either *produce the salt itself, at that custom-house* on or before the
" 5th of April thereafter, or cured fish in such quantities as
" are sufficient to exhaust the whole salt, which fish, he is obliged
" to declare upon oath were cured with the salt for which he
" had granted bond. It is only after all these forms, *and several*
" *others* are duly complied with, that the bond can be got up;
" and these bonds if not cancelled *before they fall due*, must be
" regularly returned to the commissioners of salt duties, by
" whom an action must be *instantly* commenced in the court of
" exchequer, for recovery of the penalties incurred in the bonds.
" If any of this salt remains unused, a new bond on the same
" terms, must be granted for it, however small the quantity
" may be, nor can that salt be moved from the place where it
" is once lodged, without an express warrant from the custom-

* Report p. 41.
† On Scots salt, the duty is one shilling and six pence per bushel, on foreign
salt ten shillings. The latter is chiefly consumed by the busses.

E

" houfe, and another bond granted by the proprietor, fpecifying,
" under heavy penalties, where it is to be landed ; which bond
" can only be withdrawn in confequence of a certificate from
" the cuftom-houfe fpecifying that it was there lodged. Nor
" can it be fhifted from one veffel to another, did both veffels
" even *belong to the fame perfon*, without an order from the cuf-
" tom-houfe, and a new bond granted ; nor can a fingle bufhel
" of that falt, in any circumftance, be fold without a new bond
" being granted for it, and a transfer of that quantity being
" made in the cuftom-houfe books."* This paffage paints, in
ftriking colours, the gloomy and ferocious jealoufy of Englifh
defpotifm. An eternal repetition of the word *bond*, may affure
us, that the act of parliament has been dictated by the very genius of Shylock. Thefe regulations are attended with fo much
expence, and intricacy, and fo great a hazard of ruinous penalties, that in many cafes they correfpond to an abfolute prohibition. In England, a fifherman grants bond but *once* ;† a diftinction that afcertains the pitiful malevolence of our *fifter*
kingdom. To give a proper comprehenfion of all the clogs
with which the Scots fifheries, and *they only* are burdened, would
require feveral fheets of paper. A few particulars may ferve
at prefent, as a fpecimen of the reft.

" If a veffel containing falt is loft at fea, or at the fifhing, proof
" muft be made of its being fo loft, before the falt bond can be re-
" covered ; and in fome cafes, the commiffioners are fo fcru-
" pulous with refpect to this proof, as to render it next to
" impoffible to recover the bond, or avoid the penalty it con-
" tains."‡ Thefe bonds coft, each of them, feven fhillings and
fix pence. As an inftance of the rigour of the commiffioners,
Dr. Anderfon tells the following ftory.

A bufs on the fifhing ftation was caft away. The mafter
went to a juftice of peace in the neighbourhood, and made
oath to the lofs of his veffel, with the falt, &c. on board, *but
not having faved his papers*, he committed a miftake of five or fix
bufhels in ftating the quantity of falt. His depofition, figned
by the juftice, was tranfmitted to the commiffioners, for recovery of the falt bond. On account of the *error*, it was returned,
to be altered. The man then went before two juftices, and made
oath to the *exact* quantity. This depofition was tranfmitted ;
but returned again as infufficient, for the law requires that it
fhould be made before a quorum of juftices *at their quarter
feffions*. By this time, the fhip-mafter had gone to fea to the
fifhery. Dr. Anderfon adds, that it was *a thoufand to one* if he

---

* Report by Dr. Anderfon, page 35.
† Illuftrations of the report, page 178.
‡ Ibid, p. 174.

had not either to pay the penalty of his bond, or lose a season of the fishing; as he could not, when at sea, be certain of attending at the precise day of the quarter sessions.* Such is the treatment of a shipwrecked mariner from Scots commissioners of salt duties! When this transaction happened, the *sympathetic* Dr. Adam Smith was a member of that quintumvirate, who sway the sceptre of salt excise in North-Britain.

"No vessel can lend or give salt to any other at the fishing or "otherwise, even though *belonging to the same owners*, because the "quantity shipped *per* cocquet in any vessel must be regularly "landed at some custom-house or other, either in fish or not used; "and if it must be lent, must be so landed and *bonded*, and again "shipped *per* cocquet anew. If lent otherwise, the salt and ves- "sel are seizable."† This author observes, that a bare list of the prosecutions, which have been raised in Scotland, on account of the salt tax, would excite horror. The most trifling mistake, in point of form, is sufficient for reducing an industrious family to beggary; yet in England, when the committee of fisheries required a list of the prosecutions that had been raised in that country since the institution of this law, the return was only ONE.‡

In consequence of so harsh a system, salt is smuggled in immense quantities from Ireland, where the duty is but three-pence *per* bushel. A person confessed, that, in a single year, he imported into one of the western islands, *nine hundred and seventy tons of salt*, which are equal to *thirty-eight thousand eight hundred and ninety bushels*. Several other people in the same island followed that trade.§ If the formalities on the remission of salt duties, did not defeat the whole intention of the law, there could be no temptation to this traffic. Dr. Anderson affirms, as a certain fact, that *five hundred thousand people* in Scotland use no salt but that of Ireland. He tells us also, on the subject of custom-house duties, in general, that he once paid thirteen shillings for leave to send coast-ways forty shillings worth of oat-meal.‖ Though the customs, in the nine most northern counties of Scotland, cannot defray the expence of collecting them, yet they are in themselves, very exorbitant, when compared with the value of the commodities on which they are paid. Bonds, certificates, and other trash of that kind, cost as much on a small cargo, as on a large one. Dr. Anderson was assured, that in the Hebrides "the expence of the custom-house officer to discharge a cargo "of coals, amounts, in many cases, to *more than four times the* "*duty on the coals*, and if the cargo be *small*, it will sometimes "*double the prime cost*."¶ The officer is to be brought from a distance of perhaps thirty miles, at an expence which the par-

* Illustrations of the report, page 175.
† Ibid p. 176.   ‡ Ibid, p. 191.   § Report. pag 47.
‖ Introduction, p. 67.   ¶ Ibid, p. 32.

ties must always defray out of their own pockets. This information explains another of his assertions, that those poor people, the Scots Highlanders, " pay at least *five hundred per cent.* more " than the merchants in London, Liverpool, or Bristol, would " have paid for the same goods."§

The subject of the Scots fisheries has already extended to some length. It shall be resumed and closed in the next chapter. For the sake of variety, and as a relief to the feelings of the reader, let us, for the present, make a short excursion into the more elevated regions of legislative iniquity.

Some people are in the habit of revering an act of parliament, as though it were the production of a superior being. To this class of readers may be recommended a perusal of the following anecdote. In summer 1789, when the bill for an excise on the manufacture of tobacco, was brought up to the house of peers, the Lord Chancellor Thurlow " treated the enacting part " of it with a high degree of mixed asperity and contempt. He " said, that the vexatious precautions and preventive security " of the excise laws, were *unnecessarily* extended to the subject " in question ; that a fit attention had not been paid to the " *essential interests and property of the manufacturers ;* that the " greater part of the enacting clauses were *absurd, contradictory,* " *ungrammatical, and unintelligible !* He expressed his wishes, " that the house of commons, if they meant to persevere in " their claim of having money bills returned from the house " of peers unaltered, would not insult them, by requiring their " adoption of laws *that would disgrace school boys.*"¶ He accordingly moved for an amendment, which was rejected by a majority of *ten* voices against *seven.* *So notably was the business of the nation attended !* The house of peers consisted at that time, including bishops, of about two hundred and fifty-nine members, so that this was just like one juryman presuming to do the office of fifteen. The bill however had been so wretchedly constructed, that an alteration appearing absolutely necessary, was urged a second time by the Duke of Richmond and carried. But before this could be accomplished, the parliament were just rising. The house of commons had not time to think of their pretended constituents. The alterations were suppressed, and the bill, with all its imperfections on its head, was discharged on the devoted tobacconists of Britain. If that parliament had been selected from the cells of Newgate, they could not have acted, in this affair, with a more atrocious contempt for every part of their duty.

§ Introduction p. 66.
|| This expression intimates, that in the opinion of Thurlow, tobacco is an improper object of excise. He was in the right ; for the tax produced a scene of stupendous injustice. A full account of it shall be given hereafter.
¶ Dodsley's Annual Register, for 1789, p. 157.

There is no greater abfurdity in what is called our conftitution than this, that the mere fhreds and ballaft of a Britifh parliament have often executed, or betrayed its moft important duties. The houfe of commons confifts of five hundred and fifty-eight perfons, including the forty-five make-weight Scots members. Of all thefe, forty form a quorum, and an hundred, or even fifty or fixty, have frequently tranfacted the moft interefting affairs. In the new conftitution of the united ftates of America, a very obvious and a very effectual remedy has been provided againft this abufe. By the fifth fection of the firft article, it is enacted, that " a majority of each houfe fhall conftitute " a quorum to do bufinefs." The conftitution of America is not like ours, a dream floating through the libraries of lawyers, and the imaginations of unprincipled place-hunters. It has been reduced to an inftrument of only ten or fifteen pages, compofed by men of fenfe, and on a fubject which they had ftudied and digefted. We return to *the Queen of Ifles.*

In the reign of William the third, one Tilly obtained an act of parliament to enable Bromfhill, an infant, to fell his intereft in the Fleet prifon ; which intereft was purchafed by Tilly. A report was fometime after made in the houfe of commons, which contains thefe words. " Mr. Pocklington, from the committee " on the abufes of prifons, &c. among a variety of other matter, " reported to the houfe, that one Brunfhill, a folicitor, had in- " formed the faid committee, that Tilly, as he was informed, " fhould fay, that he obtained that act *by bribery and corruption.*

" That one Mrs. Hancock applying to Tilly not to protect one " Guy, being his clerk of the papers, becaufe he was perjured, " &c. Tilly refufed her requeft ; upon which, being afked how " he would do, if the matter fhould be laid before parliament ? " he replied, *he could do what he would there;* that they were *a* " *company of bribed villains;* that to his knowledge, they would " *all take bribes;* and that it coft him three hundred pounds for " his fhare, and three hundred pounds for the other fhop, mean- " ing the King's Bench, for *bribing a committee laft parliament.*

" That fhe then intimated that fhe muft then apply to the " houfe of lords ; he anfwered, it was only *palming five or fix* " *talking lords,* and they would quafh all the reft. And fhe then " faid, fhe would try the king and council ; he added, the beft " of the lord-keeper's fees were from *him;* that as to the judges, " they were all fuch a parcel of rogues, that *they would fwallow* " *his gold* fafter than he would give it them ; and that as to the " members of the houfe of commons, they were many of them " *members of his houfe.*" * This picture feems unfavourable; but the parliaments of William the third were chiefly compofed of

* On the ufe and abufe of parliaments, vol. I. p. 126.

very exceptionable characters. An example or two as to their general conduct may serve at present.

In 1694, William planned an expedition against Brest. The particulars were betrayed to James the second, by letters from England. In consequence of this intelligence, the French prepared for the reception of their assailants. A body of English land forces were disembarked at Brest. They perceived such formidable entrenchments, and batteries, that they attempted to retreat on board their ships. But the tide had gone out; the flat bottomed boats were entangled in the mud; and the French, with superior forces, poured from every side upon the fugitives. Six hundred of those who landed were slain, and many wounded; one Dutch frigate was sunk, after losing almost her whole crew. General Talmarsh, commander in the expedition, died of his wounds at Plymouth. Sir John Dalrymple, in attempting to describe the particulars of this transaction, seems to labour under an idea of guilt and infamy, which the weakness of human language is incapable of expressing. He says, that the " intention " was betrayed to the late king, by intelligence in the spring from " Lord Godolphin, first Lord of the Treasury, and afterwards " by a letter from Lord Marlborough, eldest lieutenant-general " in the service, of date the 4th of May, in the same way as " a project against Toulon *was betrayed two years afterwards* " *by Lord Sunderland.*"[*] The letter from Marlborough was transmitted to France by Sackfield, a British major-general. A copy of it has been published by Mr. Macpherson.[+] In this epistle, Marlborough complains, that Russel, though he knew the plan, *always denied it.* " This," said he, " gives me a bad sign of this " man's intentions." His fears were groundless, for Russel himself was in a private correspondence with James, who had given instructions " to him, the Duke of Leeds, the Lords Shrews- " bury, Godolphin and Marlborough, *and others*, to create de- " lays in the fitting out of the fleet."[‡] Talmarsh, or Talmache, for his name is differently spelt, had himself once been in private connections with the friends of James, and when dying, complained, that he had fallen by the treachery of his countrymen.[||] The facts stated in this narrative are authenticated by the correspondence of the parties, which is still extant in the hand writings of some of themselves.[§] Russel " and others," might as well have cut the throats of Talmache and his men, in Smithfield market. About the end of the reign of Queen Anne, Har-

---

[*] Memoirs of Great-Britain and Ireland, Part III. Book 3d.
[+] State Papers, quarto edition, vol. 1. page 487.
[‡] Memoirs of Great Britain and Ireland, Part III. Book 3d.
[||] Ibid.
[§] The instructions by James about retarding the expedition to Brest, are published by Mr. Macpherson in his State Papers, vol. 1. p. 456.

ley, Earl of Oxford, found it convenient to pretend an attachment to the family of Stuart. He obtained the original letter
from Marlborough to James the second ; and as the Duke had
begun to be troublesome, Harley gave him notice that this letter had been procured, and consequently that his life was in danger. The Duke immediately retired from England. * His share
in betraying the Brest expedition is less criminal than a practice
urged against him by Earl Pawlet, who once told him to his face
in the house of peers, " that he sacrificed his officers in despe-
" rate assaults, *for the sake of selling their commissions.*" † This was
the *great* Duke of Marlborough, for such we continue to call
him. In the landing of the British troops at Brest, the Marquis
of Caermarthen behaved with great bravery, while his own father, Lord Caermarthen, was along with Russel and Co. betraying the country.

The following detail exhibits perfidy of a different species. In
1696, the public credit of England had sunk very greatly. To
relieve it, parliament, by the persuasion of Mr. Montague, chancellor of the exchequer, permitted him to issue exchequer bills
to the extent of two millions and seven hundred thousand pounds.
To encourage the currency of these bills, " it had been provid-
" ed, that from the date of their being paid upon taxes into the
" exchequer, they should be entitled to seven and an half per
" cent. of interest." ‡ The legal interest of money was that time.
six per cent. To raise the interest of a bill by one and an half, it
was only requisite that he holder should indorse it to some friend,
who would present it at a custom-house or excise office, and then,
through its merit in having circulated, the next indorsee, who
accepted it from the exchequer was entitled, instead of six, to
the seven and an half per cent. of interest. This appears to have
been the scope of the scheme. The process was plain and profitable ; and if Montague had been ambitious of transforming
the whole British nation into paper-jobbers, he could not have
devised a more dexterous expedient. We may be quite certain
that every bill, when first issued from the exchequer, would re
turn with the velocity of lightning. But the most beautiful part
of the transaction is yet in reserve. " Mr. Duncombe, and Mr.
" Knight. Receiver-General of the Excise, both members of
" *the house*, and others like them, officers of the revenue, put
" false endorsements on many of the bills before they had been
" circulated at all ; by which Duncombe acquired a fortune of
" *four hundred thousand pounds*." ‖ The sum is either exaggerated,
or the value of the exchequer bills must have exceeded two mil

* Memoirs of Great-Britain and Ireland, Part III. Book 3d.
† Smollet s History of Queen Anne.
‡ Memoirs of Great-Britain and Ireland, Part III. Book 4.
‖ Ibid.

lions and feven hundred thoufand pounds, for even on *the whole*
of the latter fum, a profit of one and an half per cent. comes
only to forty thoufand five hundred pounds. Perhaps Duncombe
and his affociates had been guilty of other practices of the fame
kind, and his fhare of the total plunder may have amounted to
four hundred thoufand pounds. " It was proved that he had
" owned the truth of the *complaint*. (A very gentle kind of term
" for forgery.) They (Knight and Duncombe) were both ex-
" pelled the houfe, and a bill paffed the commons to fine Mr.
" Duncombe (in) half his eftate; but it was rejected in the houfe
" of lords by the cafting vote of the Duke of Leeds." About
two years before, this ineftimable peer had been impeached by
the houfe of commons for receiving, from the governors of the
Eaft-India company, a bribe of five thoufand guineas. This money had been kept for about a year and an half; and, according
to evidence, delivered at the bar of the houfe, it was then returned to the witnefs, " becaufe the Duke's fervant's getting it was
" *making a noife.*" * This nobleman was at that very time lord pre-
fident of his majefty's moft honourable privy council, and betraying to James the fecond the project of the Breft expedition.
We need not then fcruple much to believe Sir John Dalrymple,
when he fays, that, in the cafe of Duncombe, " *private* money
" was fufpected to have had influence with a number of the
" peers." Lord Chefterfield had fome reafon for terming that
houfe an hofpital of *incurables*. By the ftatute law of England,
Duncombe, and all his confederates, ought to have fuffered
death; but it is difficult to hang a man with four hundred thoufand pounds in his pocket.

In 1695, Sir John Fenwick, a major-general, had been engaged with fome others, in a project for a rebellion in England,
and had, on its difcovery, fled. Some time after he returned, was
found out, and arrefted. To fave his life, he tranfmitted to
William an account of the treafonable correfpondence of Go-
dolphin, Marlborough, Ruffel, and other *whigs of diftinction*
with James. His accufation " is now known to have been in all
" points *true*;" and as there was only *one* evidence againft him,
of his fhare in the confpiracy, " he could not be convicted in a
" court of law, which required *two*." William was thoroughly
acquainted with the real character of the perfons thus accufed by
Fenwick; but he durft not come to an open rupture with fuch
powerful offenders. The charge was therefore fmothered; but
the perfons, whom Fenwick had accufed, " believed that they
" could not be fafe *as long as he lived*." A bill of attainder was
therefore brought into parliament againft him, and his late friend
Ruffel appeared at the head of the profecution. The bill paft

---

* Memoirs of Great Britain and Ireland, Part iii. Book 3.

through the house of commons by an hundred and eighty-nine
voices against an hundred and fifty-six. In the upper house, it
had only a majority of seven. Gilbert Burnet, that *right reve-
rend father in God*, by a long speech, " exhausted all the chica-
" nery of the law, and all the *hypocrisy of the church*, to vindi-
" cate proceedings, which exceeded the injustice of the worst
" precedents of Charles the second, and his successor. But by
" a mixture of vanity and shame, although he inserted the speech
" in his history, he did not avow that he was the person who
" made it." On the 28th of January, 1696, Sir John Fenwick,
was, " *without evidence or law*," beheaded on Tower-Hill. Lady
Fenwick having feared the testimony of a person, she attempted to bribe him to fly the kingdom. The accusers directed this
wretch to place people behind a curtain to overhear the offer;
" and this attempt of a wife to save her husband's life from dan-
" ger, *was turned into an evidence of his guilt*."* These are the
words of an historian, who is himself a professed *whig*, who has
been a lawyer, and is now a judge. It appears, therefore, that
in the close of the last century, the majority of a British parliament committed a deliberate murther; and that they did so under the pretence of punishing a conspirator, while, at the same
time, a considerable number of themselves were partners in his
guilt. Contrasted with so black a scene, there is nothing remarkable in the ruin of British tobacconists, or in the accusation so
bluntly advanced by the keeper of the Fleet-prison. The king
himself, when he consented to this bill, must have been altogether conscious of its criminality; but specks of that kind cannot
tarnish the purity of so luminous a character.

Since the Norman conquest, England has been governed, including Oliver Cromwell, by thirty-three sovereigns; and of
these, two-thirds were, each of them, by an hundred different
actions, deserving of the gibbet.† Yet the people, over whom
they ruled, seem to have been, for the most part, quite worthy
of such masters, and to have been as perfectly divested of every
honourable feeling, *as majesty itself*. In evidence of this truth, let
us examine the history of a circumstance in the reign of Charles
the second, that provoked more than usual indignation. At that
time, there existed no national debt; but when the parliament
had voted supplies, it was common for bankers, and wealthy individuals, to advance money to the exchequer, on the faith of

* Memoirs of Great-Britain and Ireland, Part III. Book 7.
† Edward II. Richard II. and Henry VI. appear to have been peaceable men.
They were all murdered. Edward Vth is supposed, when a boy, to have shared
the same fate. Of Edward VI. the exit is not free from suspicion. Queen Anne
was, upon the whole, a harmless woman; and every Englishman acknowledges
with gratitude and with pride, that the virtues of the house of Brunswick tran-
scend all praise.

F

repayment, when the produce of the grants thus voted came into the public treafury. On the 2d of January, 1672, the exchequer was indebted to the bankers and others in the amount of one million, three hundred and twenty-eight thoufand, five hundred and twenty-fix pounds; and on this day, Charles fufpended payment. A bankruptcy, for ten times that fum, would not affect, with an equal degree of ruin, the prefent commerce of England. The king, however, charged his hereditary revenue with the legal intereft of this fum at fix *per cent.* and this was actually and regularly paid, till about a year before his death, when it was ftopped. As he advanced the intereft with punctuality for fo long a time, we may candidly judge that his failure in the end arofe from neceffity. Sir John Sinclair fays, that the fhutting up of the exchequer "will for ever ftamp the character of "Charles the fecond with *the moft indelible infamy.*"* His character was, upon a thoufand other emergencies, fo completely *ftamped*, that any fingle crime could have added little to the accompt. But the point in queftion is to prove, that in this very affair, Charles, bad as he was, behaved with greater honefty than *any body elfe*. Nay, he pofitively acted with ten thoufand times more regard to juftice than Lord Somers, who is commonly reputed to have been the moft virtuous and immaculate perfonage in the fanctified corps of revolution whigs. When Charles could no longer pay the intereft of the money, the unfortunate creditors attempted, but in vain, to intereft the legiflature in their behalf. "They "were at laft obliged to maintain their rights in the courts of "juftice. The fuit was protracted for *about twelve years* in the "courts below, but judgment was obtained againft the crown, "about the year 1697. The decifion, however, was fet afide by "Lord Somers, then chancellor; though it is faid that tèn out "of the twelve judges, whom he had called to his affiftance were "of a different opinion. The caufe was at laft carried by appeal "to the houfe of lords, by whom the decree of the chancellor "was reverfed; and the patentees would of courfe have receiv- "ed *the annual intereft contained in the original letters patent,* had "not an act paffed *anno* 1699, by which, in lieu thereof, it was "enacted, that after the 25th of December, 1705, the heredi- "tary revenue of excife fhould ftand charged with the annual "payment of THREE *per cent.* for the principal fum contained in "the faid letters patent, fubject neverthelefs to be redeemed "upon the payment of a moiety thereof, or fix hundred and "fixty-four thoufand, two hundred and fixty-three pounds."†

The good people of Britain fpeak with as much fluency of French and Spanifh treachery, as if we had engroffed in our own

---

* Hiftory of the public revenue, part ii. chap. 3.
† Ibid.

persons the whole integrity of the human race. Yet it will be difficult to find a single transaction, in any age, that more thoroughly blackens the character of an entire nation than the robbery of these creditors. The perfidy of Charles himself is forgot in the superior blaze of subsequent scoundrelism. First, the flaming parliamentary patriots of that time refused to trouble themselves about the matter; though *their* piety was so deeply alarmed by the prospect of a Popish successor to the crown. In the second place, the claim became a question in *the courts below*. That the re-payment of this thirteen hundred thousand pounds should ever have been an object of hesitation at all, was, in itself, an utter disgrace to the whole system of English jurisprudence. The law-suit lasted for *twelve years*. During this time, and while the court of London rolled in luxury, many of the creditors must have gone to jail, or at least, many subordinate creditors, whom the former, in consequence of this fraud, were unable to satisfy. An immense number of families must have been reduced to beggary; and a croud of honest fathers and husbands must have died of a broken heart. At length a decision was obtained, and approved by ten out of the twelve judges. The creditors were to receive the annual interest of their money. Why they should not have been warranted to recover the principal sum itself, must remain among other secrets of the deep. A thousand racked bankrupts rejoiced in the prospect of restitution.

Till at the last, a cruel spoiler came,
Crops this fair flower, and rifled all its sweetness.

The decision was reversed by Somers, the lord chancellor, a sage, who exhibited in his own person the very focus of whig virtue.* This conduct reminds us of the proverb, that *the receiver is as bad as the thief*. Charles paid the interest of the money as long as he could. Somers would pay nothing. It is therefore indisputable that, of the two rogues, the *receiver* was in this instance, by much the greater. The house of lords reversed so scandalous a decree, but mark what follows. An act of parliament was immediately passed, which, in opposition to every

* "One of those divine men, who, like a chapel in a palace, remain unpro-
"phaned, while all the rest is tyranny, corruption, and folly. All the tradition-
"al accounts of him, the historians of the last age, and its best authors, repre-
"sent him as the *most incorrupt lawyer* and *the honestest statesman*; as a master orator,
"a genius of the finest taste, and as a patriot of the noblest and most extensive
"views; as a man, who dispensed blessings by his life, and planned them for
"posterity." Catalogue of royal and noble authors by Horace Walpole. Art.
SOMERS. The writer proceeds in a rhapsody of five pages to the same purpose.
He appeals to the historians and *the best authors* of the last age. It is likely that none
of these encomiasts had been creditors to the English exchequer, in the reign of
Charles the second. But the panegyrics of all mankind cannot convert an act of
arrant robbery into an act of justice. The historians to whom Mr Walpole appeals, prove nothing but how vilely the British annals have commonly been composed.

principle of law, of juftice, and of decency, interfered with the
decifion of a judicial court. To confummate the infamy of the
Englifh houfe of peers, they confented as *legiflators*, to the re-
verfal of their own decifion as *judges*, thus demonftrating their
invulnerable contempt for all veftige of reputation. In the end,
payment was delayed for more than five additional years, and
then, the *half* of the legal intereft was begun to be paid annually, but redeemable on refunding *half* of the fum originally ftolen. The reader will obferve in what kind of milk and
water ftyle Sir John Sinclair has related this ftory. He has made
a fubfequent but fmall miftake, in faying that the creditors were
kept for *twenty-five* years out of their money. From a year before the death of Charles the fecond,* to the 25th of December, 1705, is a period of lefs than twenty-*three* years. At fix *per
cent.* of compound intereft, a fum doubles itfelf once in eleven
years, and three hundred and thirty-one days, or twice, in twenty-three years and about ten months. For the fake of round
numbers, let us reduce the original debt to thirteen hundred
thoufand pounds, and fuppofe that it doubled *twice* during the
time when payment of intereft was fufpended. At this rate, the
merchants had in December, 1705, loft five millions and two
hundred thoufand pounds fterling, befides their expences in a
law-fuit of twelve years. In compenfation, parliament granted
them an annuity of three *per cent.* on the original fum, that is
to fay, *thirty-nine thoufand eight hundred and fifty-five pounds, feventeen fhillings and feven pence fterling.* At fix *per cent.* the annual intereft of five millions and two hundred thoufand pounds
amounted to three hundred and twelve thoufand pounds. Thus
parliament gave fomewhat more than an *eighth* part of what the
merchants had actually loft. We now fee that the felonious ravages of an Englifh government are not reftricted to Scots Highlanders. With fuch a gulph of iniquity yawning on every fide,
we are tempted to think ourfelves perufing the Tyburn Chronicle. The real caufe for fhutting up the exchequer was yet more
difreputable than the act itfelf. Charles had declared war againft
the Dutch, for the fame reafon that a Dey of Algiers declares
it.† The conteft had coft more than five millions fterling. His
parliament refufed to relieve him from the preffure of fome of

* He died on the 6th of February, 1684.
† " The wars which the king entered into againft the Dutch, were principal-
" ly with a view *of plundering a wealthy*, and, as he imagined, a *defencelefs* neigh-
" bour." Hiftory of the public revenue, part 1. chap. 9. The war, begun by the
commonwealth of England againft Holland, in 1652, was likewife unprovoked
by the latter. In thefe three quarrels more lives were loft, and more mifchief
done, than has been committed by all the corfairs of Barbary ever fince, and
yet we pretend to call thefe people *pirates*, while the far more extenfive enormities of the Britifh navy, are burnifhed into pages of heroifm. In the practice of
fea-robbery England has exceeded every other nation. Vid. fome account of
thefe three wars, infra. chap. 6th.

the expences. The king offered to make any man treasurer, who would remove his necessities. Clifford embraced the proposal, and the exchequer was closed. The Dutch wars were infinitely more criminal than even this action, but these were only piracies abroad ; the other was piracy at *home* ; and for that reason only has it been condemned. In 1655, Oliver Cromwell, without either provocation or pretence, attacked Spain ; and we still celebrate the Algerine victories of admiral Blake over the fleets of that injured country, which proves that the nation has not yet acquired more wisdom or honesty, than its ancestors. A very modern example of profligacy shall close this chapter.

Sixty thousand pounds were granted by parliament to George the Third, that he might be enabled to make an establishment for his eldest son. Fifty thousand pounds a year were likewise bestowed upon this young man for his personal expences. An hundred and eighty-one thousand pounds have since been assigned by parliament for his works at Carleton-house, and for the discharge of debts which he had contracted notwithstanding his pension of fifty thousand pounds a year.† Ten thousand pounds *per annum*, like a drop in the bucket, were also added to his allowance, that he might never be under the necessity of incurring new debts. It is said, however, that the sum thus entrusted, was never applied to the discharge of his debts ; and at least one circumstance is certain, that the prince of Wales continues to be on the wrong side of the hedge, by many hundred thousands of pounds. A gentleman, who had the best access to information, hath privately stated them to be at least a million sterling. It is reported, that great numbers of London tradesmen have been compelled to shut up their shops, in consequence of their unfortunate connection with this bankrupt. His stud of horses has more than once been sold for much less than these animals originally cost him. The task of recording his exploits, must be reserved for the pen of some future Suetonius. At the present time (September, 1792,) it may be safely computed, that in one shape or other, he has expended for the nation eight hundred thousand pounds sterling. We may compare this mode of exhausting the public treasury, with that employed in the highlands of Scotland to replenish it.

On a subject so hateful, there can be no pleasure to expatiate. Indeed, the taste of the nation runs in a very opposite channel. We can hardly open a newspaper, without meeting a rhapsody on the virtues and abilities of the prince of Wales. His admirers, like the spaniel that licks the foot raised to kick him, are not contented with general praise. They tell us, in transports of exultation, that he gave a thousand guineas for " **an** *admirable* snuff-

† History of the public revenue, part iii. chap. 2.

box;" that, upon a late birth-day, he appeared at court in a suit of cloaths, which, including diamonds, cost eighty thousand pounds; that he bought a race-horse for fifteen hundred guineas, and sold him for seventy pounds; that he was present sometime ago at a boxing match, where a shoemaker was struck dead with a single blow; and that he drove a lady round St. James's Park, or that she drove him, no matter which, in a phaeton, with four black ponies.†

For these inestimable services, the nation has paid eight hundred thousand pounds; a sum lost in the bottomless pit of Carleton house. How many future millions are, like Curtius, to be swallowed up in the same gulph, time only can determine. Since this country had the honor of establishing a household for the prince of Wales, we have been burdened with additional taxes upon snuff and tobacco, on paper, advertisements, leather, perfumery, horses, attornies, batchelors, stage-coaches, gloves, hats, male and female servants,‡ pedlars and shop-keepers; upon windows, candles, medicines, bills and receipts; upon newspapers and partridges; and if any thing can be yet more impertinent or oppressive, on births, burials and legacies; besides other impositions beyond the retention of perhaps the strongest memory. Now, it is remarkable, that ten of these taxes might be selected, which, by their nett produce, could not, in whole, have discharged the expences of this single private person. We are incessantly deafened about our obligations to the house of Guelph. It would be but candid to state an estimate of their obligations to us, and to strike the balance.

In North-America, there are sometimes found the bones of a carniverous quadruped, which must have been, when alive, three or four times larger than the elephant. This animal, which may likely have been amphibious, appears now to be extirpated. Perhaps it perished from an impossibility of obtaining adequate subsistence. A forest thirty leagues in length would have been insufficient to furnish food for so formidable a guest. It is possible that *the species of kings* may, one day, come to be extirpated for a similar reason. The gluttony of the mammoth, devouring six buffaloes for a breakfast, bears no proportion to the ordinary

† It is very generally whispered and believed, that an *illustrious* personage shot one of his footmen dead with a pistol, for disrespect to a woman. If this be true, the life of Dr. Philip Withers has not been the only sacrifice at that shrine; nor will Morocco be in future, the only country in the world governed by an executioner.

In the London Chronicle, I read, many years ago, an article stating, that a very young naval officer, *whose name was inserted at full length*, had stabbed one of his servants. There was never any farther notice in the newspapers of this story; but I have since learned, that the man died of his wound; and that a sailor on board of the ship where the murder was committed, underwent a sham trial for it, and was discharged.

‡ The latter tax ought to have been entitled a receipe for female idleness, theft and prostitution.

extent of royal rapacity. Two hundred families of fovereigns, like thofe of France or England, would, of themfelves, be fufficient for confuming the whole revenues of Europe.

In the courfe of a century, from the revolution to Michaelmas, 1788, the pilots of our moft excellent conftitution, have received into the Britifh exchequer, one thoufand millions, fix hundred and forty-four thoufand, one hundred and fifty-four pounds fterling.* It will be hard to prove, that even a twentieth part of this money has been expended on wife or ufeful purpofes. To this we muft add the charge of collecting the revenue for the fame period, which, on a medium, can be guefled at fix hundred thoufand pounds *per annum*. This rate extends, in an hundred years, to fixty millions of pounds fterling, deburfed for the invaluable exploits of cuftom-houfe and excife officers. Such a fum, at a compound intereft of five *per cent.* computing from the refpective dates of its annual expenditure, would, by this time, have been large enough to buy up, in fee fimple, the Britifh iflands, with the laft acre, and the laft guinea that they contain.

CHAPTER II.

Fertility of the Hebrides—Iflay—Its prodigious improvement—Immenfe abundance of fifh—Miferable effects of excife—Salt and coal duties—Specimen of Scots finecures.

WE have, in the laft chapter, learned fome of the circumftances that prevent the improvement of Scots fifheries. We fhall now return to that fubject, by a farther examination of Dr. Anderfon's performance. Other writers have caft light on this queftion, and well deferve to be quoted. But the prefent work embraces an immenfe multiplicity of objects ; and hence, it becomes requifite to condenfe and abridge our materials. There is not to be expected, in this place, a complete account of the fituation of the inhabitants in the northern counties, and in the iflands of Scotland. A few interefting facts only will be ftated ; fome fhocking abufes of government will be exhibited ; and fome obvious reflections will be fubmitted to the public. By a fketch of this kind, the fpirit of curiofity and of enquiry may perhaps be excited ; and then every perfon is able, at his own convenience, to make himfelf mafter of the cafe. This may be refolved into three points, the natural advantages of the country itfelf, the miferable confequences refulting from the tyranny of parliament, and the numerous benefits that would arife from an honeft and beneficent adminiftration.

* Hiftory of the public revenue, part III. chap. I.

It has commonly been supposed, that the Hebrides were barren and unfit for agriculture. On the contrary, Dr. Anderson states, that they contain extensive fields of unusual fertility. Many tracts which have never been ploughed are capable to produce corn, and to supply subsistence for a multitude of people. Arran excepted, which is very mountainous, the western islands are for the most part level. Tiree, for example, is one continued plain of fine arable land, with only two small hills. The west side of Barra, of Uist, and of Harris, and the whole of the islands between these, as well as the north-west side of Lewis, are low lands. They are one entire bed of shell-sand, and extremely fruitful. Dr. Anderson, who is himself a farmer of experience, observes, that the fields of shell-sand, when well cultivated, and properly manured with sea-weed, give crops of barley, which cannot, as he imagines, be equalled in any part of Europe. He adds, that were he to specify the particulars, they would not obtain credit. The crops of pease and rye are very luxuriant : and he supposes that turnips, lucerne, sainfoin, and wheat, might be raised in as great perfection there, as any where in this quarter of the world. Lime-stone, marl, and shell-sand, *are every where to be met with in great plenty.* The islands of Cannay and Egg, consist of several rows of basaltic columns raised one above each other. The ground is not level, but the soil is very fertile. The rocks of Lismore consist entirely of lime-stone, and the land is fruitful, even to a proverb. The climate of the western islands is more favourable, and the harvest for the most part more early than on the opposite coast of Scotland. During summer, the wind blows commonly from the south-west, and of consequence it is loaded with clouds from the Atlantic. The high lands on the western coasts intercept these clouds, and the rain descends in torrents. But in the islands the ground is low. The clouds pass over them without obstruction. There is usually less rain in summer than the inhabitants would desire. The harvest is more early and more certain than on the continent. In Islay, the crops are commonly secured before the end of September ; a more early season than in East Lothain, the best corn country of Scotland. Among the western islands, where the soil is not shell-sand, the surface very frequently consists of mossy earth. When manured with shell-sand, it becomes at once capable of bearing excellent crops of grain. When afterwards laid into grass, it becomes covered with a fine swaird, consisting chiefly of white clover and the poa-grasses ; so that this improved soil becomes in future equally adapted for corn or pasture. Those hills, which cannot be ploughed, are yet susceptible of the greatest improvement. When covered with that sort of manure which is every where plentiful and inexhaustible, they immediately obtain a fine pile of delicate and perennial grass.

As an evidence of what may be accomplished in the Hebrides, by the joint efforts of industry and judgment, we may consider the proceedings of Walter Campbell, Esquire, of Shawfield, proprietor of Islay. About twelve years before Dr. Anderson came to visit it, this island, like most of the Hebrides, at present, had no roads on which carriages could be drawn, no bridges, no public work of any kind. It contained less than seven thousand people ; and it imported annually, between three and four thousand bolls of grain. Thus, if shut out from the rest of the world, the inhabitants must have expired of hunger. They were discontented ; and they had begun to emigrate. Their departure was interrupted by the very judicious war against America, which commenced for a duty of three pence per pound upon tea, and terminated with an expence of one hundred and thirty-nine millions sterling. Now, let us consider the state of this island in the year 1785. In spite of the intervention of a bloody war, that lasted for seven years and an half out of the twelve, and checked all sorts of improvement in all parts of the empire, the population had augmented to ten thousand souls. These, instead of importing their subsistence, exported annually, about five thousand bolls of grain, three thousand six hundred head of black cattle, between three and four hundred horses, and about thirty-six thousand spindles of yarn, all of their own produce and manufacture. Thirty miles of excellent roads had already been formed. A great number of useful bridges were erected. A well-constructed pier had been built. A town was begun ; and its inhabitants multiplied with rapidity. Markets were opened for the produce of the land. Large tracts of barren ground were annually brought into culture. The people were industrious and satisfied. This rapid improvement was atchieved, in a poor and sequestered island, by the exertions of a single private gentleman.*
Hence, it seems evident, that if the rest of Scotland had been governed with equal wisdom, its wealth, population, importance, and felicity, must, at the same time, have increased in a similar proportion. From sixteen hundred thousand people, we should, in twelve years, have multiplied to two millions and three hundred thousand. At the same time, Scotland must have

* Dr. Anderson observed to a friend, that part of the superior good sense of mr. Campbell arose from his happiness in being born a younger brother. He did not obtain the estates of the family till he had reached the maturity of his understanding ; when the death of an elder son, without children, put him into possession of them. Such is the ridiculous consequence of the right of primogeniture, that it not only half-beggars the rest of the family, but in two cases out of three, the object of its favour has a very great chance for being a blockhead. Every body may remark, at a grammar school, that heirs are in general the most idle, ignorant, and vicious of all the boys. Out of these hopeful materials our future parliaments are to be formed.

been able to export grain in much greater quantities than what she at present imports. The agriculture of the country must very soon have doubled its productions. The existence of seven hundred thousand additional people, in twelve years only, hath been prevented by the magic wands of five or six hundred custom-house and excise officers.

It is remarkable, that though the *free* government of Britain cannot perform revolutions like that effected by Mr. Campbell, yet a task of this nature has, within our own days, been executed by one of the most inflexible despots that ever menaced mankind. In the year 1763, the dominions of Frederick the Great had been reduced to the utmost distress. The king himself, in his posthumous memoirs, observes, that " no descrip-" tion, however pathetic, can possibly approach to the deep, the " afflicting, the mournful impression, which *the sight of them* " *inspired*." Among other particulars, he tells us, that they had lost *five hundred thousand inhabitants*. Thirteen thousand houses had been razed from the earth ; and the whole nation, from the noble to the peasant, were in rags that hardly covered their nakedness. In about eight years of peace, the breaches of population were perfectly repaired, and the whole country became as flourishing as ever. Thus, what Mr. Campbell acted upon a small scale, was done by Frederick upon a greater. There is no doubt that Scotland itself might be improved as quickly as the island of Islay. For instance, Dr. Anderson remarks, that within the last fifty years, a very great alteration for the better has taken place in the neighbourhood of Aberdeen. Many thousand acres of the most barren land that can be conceived, have been converted into excellent corn-fields ; and he computes that, in consequence of this change, the rent of this land has been augmented by more than thirty thousand pounds sterling *per annum*. The iron forge at Bunaw gives employment to several families. When they were planted near it, the soil was nothing but a bleak moss with some dwarfish heath. Of this land, several hundred acres are now covered with grass and corn. The steep mountain, at fort William, seemed by nature incapable of improvement ; but is now overspread with gardens and corn-fields. To these details by Dr. Anderson, every person may, from his own observation, add others of the same kind. The history of the parish of Portpatrick, in the statistical account of Scotland, affords an instance of how much may be done for a barren corner. What adds to the merit of the improvements in Islay is, that they were accomplished under the most oppressive system of taxation which can be devised. The proprietor himself has encountered the most rancorous insolence in carrying on the fishery, not only from the commissioners of the salt duties, but from a petty officer of excise ; and if, he had not been a very able and powerful man, these harpies might have reduced him to bankruptcy. We must not, therefore, complain of providence, because the Hebrides, and a considerable part of the main land of Scotland, are still in a state of comparative desolation. Industry lingers not for want of a richer soil, or a milder sky, but for want of such a legislator as Frederick sometimes was, and such landlords as Walter Campbell. It is not merely by the quality of the soil, that the Hebrides may become valuable. Mines of lead and copper have been found in Islay; and in Tyree and Skye, quarries of excellent marble have been discovered. Coal has been met with in several places, but a discovery of this nature must be useless, unless to the island where it may be dug; because the coasting duty upon coal would effectually prevent its being exported, even to the neighbouring islands. Their inhabitants live in scattered hamlets. They can buy but a small quantity of coals at one time, possibly only half a ton. The expence of bringing an excise officer for thirty miles, perhaps, to inspect the coals, an expence which the parties must pay, would often come, as before observed, to four times the price of the cargo. In the same way, if the natives had any cargo fit for a foreign market, they must, before they can sail, obtain a clearance from the custom-house. This would, in many cases, cost more than the worth of the cargo.

The circumstance by which the Hebrides have as yet been principally distinguished, is that immense quantity of excellent fish that fill the surrounding seas. It is unnecessary here to mention the names of perhaps thirty different kinds, including a great variety of shell-fish; but let us remark the idiotism of the English government, when pretending to remit the salt duties for the sake of encouraging the Scots fisheries. The persons who receive *bonded* salt are not suffered to catch any fish but herrings. They must carry their men, and boats, their nets, and salt, and casks to the fishing ground. They must remain there for three months, and if a shoal of cod or turbot, of haddocks, of mullet, of soal, of flounders, or halybut, comes in their way, they are not at liberty to take them; but are condemned to spend these three months in perfect idleness,* unless they meet with a shoal of herrings. Yet it frequently happens that, but for this prohibition, they could load their vessels with cargoes of other fish equally valuable. At the end of three months, they must bring their men, their boats, their nets, their salt, and their casks, back to the custom-house, before their salt bonds can be relieved. If there had been no other fish but herrings in the western seas, an excuse might have been made. But this is not the case. The dogfish are sometimes to be met with in such vast numbers, that their back fins are seen like a thick bush of sedges above the wa-

* Report, p. 43.

ter, as far as the eye can reach. A boat-load in such a shoal may be catched with a few hand-lines in an hour or two. A valuable oil is extracted from their liver. A fisherman at Islay informed Dr. Anderson, that he frequently baited a line with four hundred hooks, for the smaller flat-fish, and caught at one haul, three hundred and fifty. They consisted of turbot, soal, and large excellent flounders, of two or three pounds weight. As to skate and halybut, he could fill his boat with them, when he chose it, at a single haul. The quantity of herrings that sometimes approach the coast, in one body, almost exceeds belief. In 1773, a shoal came into Loch Terridon. Many hundreds of boats were loaded as oft as the owners thought proper for two months; and the quantity caught in a single night, has been computed, by Dr. Anderson, at nineteen thousand eight hundred barrels. Of the quantities brought ashore upon such occasions, a great part are frequently suffered to putrify, for want of salt to cure them. The remainder are cured exclusively with Irish salt; for, in Dr. Anderson's opinion, as already observed, five hundred thousand people in the north of Scotland employ none else. Thus, on the one hand, the heaviness of the tax defeats its own purpose, and on the other hand, as the smugglers of salt cannot obtain open leave to export their cargoes of fish, the business ends in a mere waste and destruction. What better indeed was to be expected, when the inhabitants of the western islands came under the domination of an assembly of parasites, at the distance of two hundred leagues, an assembly who despise their interests, abhor their prosperity, and are sufficiently disposed even to exterminate their language? If Galgacus had submitted to Julius Agricola, he would not have endured any such absurd despotism.

At Loch Carron, about the year 1775, herrings " were so " throng, that though the loch, from the narrow entry, is above " a league long, and in some places above a mile broad, and " from sixty to four fathoms deep, it was indifferent to the fish- " ers whether their nets were near the ground or surface; they " were equally sure to have them loaded. They continued in this " bay for five weeks. On the west side of Skye, I am informed, " they once swarmed so thick in Caroy loch, and so many were " caught, that they could not be carried off; and after the busses " were loaded, and the country round was served, *the neighbour-* " *ing farmers made them up into composts, and manured their ground* " *with them the ensuing season.* This shoal continued many years " upon the coast, but they were not in every year, nor in every " bay, so thick as this last; but were, for a number of years, so " much so, that all the busses made cargoes, and the whole coasts " were abundantly served.—At Loch Urn, in 1767, or 1768, " such a quantity *ran on shore,* that the beach, for four miles

" round the head of the loch, was covered with them, from
" fix to eighteen inches deep; and the ground under water, fo
" far as it could be feen at low water, was equally fo. I believe
" the whole bay, from the narrow to the mouth, about twelve
" miles long, and a league broad, was *full of them*. I am alfo
" of opinion, that the ftrongeft fifh being without, in forcing
" their way into the inner bay, drove the lighteft and weakeft
" on fhore. So thick were thefe laft, that they carried before
" them every other kind of fifh they met, even ground-fifh,
" fkate, flounders, &c. and perifhed together."* With fuch
inconceivable quantities of fifh at home, we can be under no
neceffity for wandering in queft of employment, to Greenland,
to Newfoundland, to Falkland's iflands, or to Nootka Sound;
and of obtaining a permiffion for fifhing fo far off, at an expence
of three millions fterling. The true caufe for fuch conduct is
fhortly this. At the union, Scotland came under the yoke of an
ancient enemy, by whom fhe was equally feared and detefted;
and no advantage to the empire in general could compenfate to
the pride of England, for the mortification of having promoted
Scots opulence.†

In the year 1784, a fhoal of herrings came into Loch Urn.
Mr. M'Donell, of Barrifdale, gave it as his opinion, that in the
courfe of feven or eight weeks, a quantity was caught, that, if
brought to market, would have fold for fifty-fix thoufand pounds
fterling. Double the quantity might have been taken, but for
the want of falt and of cafks. Were it not for the interruption
of an excife, and fome other obvious caufes, the fifhery bufinefs, in that quarter, would be more lucrative than any other that
a labouring man can follow in any part of Britain.‡

Thefe examples prove what immenfe loads of fifh might be
killed, if the people had a proper fupply of falt and of cafks for
curing them, and a fuitable market for felling them; fo that they
might be able to continue at the fifhery during the whole time
which it lafted. At prefent, the mifchief that is left undone by
the exorbitant excife upon falt, is completed by the prepofterous
terms on which the bounty is granted. When a bufs has completed her cargo, *fhe muft abandon the fifhing entirely;* **and none** of her

---

* Illuftrations of the report, p. 158.

† The prefent method of paving and lighting the ftreets of London, is, as an
improvement, felt in the moft fenfible manner by all ranks and degrees of people. The plan of this work was borrowed from the high ftreet of Edinburgh,
and the very ftones for the pavement were imported from Scotland. For the
perfonal fafety of the gentlemen concerned, and their families, thefe circumftances were concealed from the rabble with the ftricteft caution. The ferocity
of vulgar patriotifm would not have fuffered the acknowledgment of fuch an ob-
ligation to North-Britain, a country, on which they daily exhauft the vocabu-
lary of Billingfgate. Vid. Dr. **Wendeborn.**

‡ Report, p. 14.

hands can return to it again in lefs than eight or ten weeks, before which time, the people of the bufs might have catched perhaps twenty loadings, *had they been permitted to remain.*

From the complicated and oppreffive conditions upon which the bounty offered by parliament has been granted, there is ground to queftion whether a fingle penny of it has ever gone into the pockets of the fifhermen. Firft, the bounty would occafion fo great an expence to many of the more remote inhabitants of the Hebrides, that they are entirely out of the queftion. Before a native of the weftern coafts or iflands, can enter himfelf, even as a private mariner, on board one of thofe veffels, that apply for the bounty, he muft go to Greenock, Rothefay, or Campbelton, and there wait till he is engaged and muftered. If this happens at one of the two former places, he proceeds to Campbelton to be rendezvoufed. Thefe marches and countermarches confume a month or fix weeks of time, and a great deal of money. At laft he returns to the very fpot from whence he fet out.* Thus it would be impoffible for a great part of the weftern Highlanders, ever to fend a bufs on fuch a circuitous voyage, for they would be obliged to difpatch her a fecond time to the fouth, to a fecond rendezvous, and to be at the charge of her making a fecond return home. She would thus be forced to perform *four* voyages inftead of *two*. The door to the pretended bounty, that ftoney piece of bread, is, by this means, both fhut and bolted. Even to the buffes that earn it, the bounty is but a mere delufion. On the eaftern coaft of Scotland, the cuftom-houfe fees, on fitting out fuch a veffel of thirty tons, are about feven pounds. The bounty is only forty-five pounds. The time wafted in going to a place of rendezvous, before fhe fails, and at her return, coft a month of delay, and a charge of twenty pounds. Thus, more than one half of the bounty is already funk. In the fecond place, fhe is prohibited from catching any fifh but herrings. On that account fhe muft have neither lines nor hooks on board. Though furrounded by whales and dogfifh, cod, ling, mackarel, and other aquatic tribes, that follow the herrings in vaft numbers, the men in thefe veffels, when herrings do not come in their way, are kept idle for weeks together, while charges multiply on the head of the undertaker.†
A third heavy obftruction is, that all the hands in the bufs muft be muftered at the cuftom-houfe, not only before failing, but *after the veffel returns.* Thus many fifhers muft be carried back to the rendezvous, who are fuperfluous for navigating the bufs, and who would otherwife be left on the fifhing-ground till the end of the feafon; and this regulation alfo is very burdenfome to the owner. The bounty is thus utterly confumed in comply-

ing with a fyftem of regulations, more fantaftical than the con-
fulfhip of Caligula's horfe.*

Thofe Hebrideans who cannot or do not embrace the terms
of the bounty, are therefore at liberty to continue at the fifhing
as long as they pleafe. They are idle or bufy, juft as they are
fupplied with falt. When a fmuggling falt-boat arrives, they
will get **perhaps fix fhillings** *per* barrel for their herrings. As
that falt **is expended,** the price falls to five, four, three, two,
one fhilling *per* barrel, **and** fometimes to fix-pence or eight-
pence. At other times, you may purchafe a barrel of fine
frefh herrings for a fingle quid of tobacco.† A barrel contains
from fix to fixteen hundred herrings, according to their fize.

It feems needlefs to enlarge much farther on the immenfe
advantages that might be derived from this inexhauftible refource for the induftry and fubfiftence of the Scots nation. If
the bounties and taxes were at once abolifhed, and the Dutch
prohibited from interfering in the fifhery, the Hebrides and
the weftern coafts of Scotland, would, likely, in the courfe
of thirty or forty years, quadruple their prefent population.
It might with reafon be expected, that thoufands of the Dutch
mariners, who are at prefent employed in that bufinefs, would
come and fettle in the country. Multitudes would likewife
flock from different quarters of Britain. Villages of manufacturers would by **degrees** be eftablifhed, and the Hebrides
would prefent **a profpect** of **induftry,** of profperity, **and of**

---

* Foreigners unacquainted with the current ftyle of Britifh converfation, may con-
demn comparifons like that in the text. Let us hear with what reverence the legiflators of this country fpeak and think of each other.

The Earl of Buchan hath juft now publifhed the lives of Fletcher, of Salton, and
of James Thomfon. He there tells us, that he once faid to Lord Chatham, " What
" will become of poor England, that doats on the imperfections of her *pretended* con-
" ftitution ?" Chatham replied, " The gout will difpofe of me foon enough to prevent
" me from feeling the confequences of this *infatuation ;* but, *before the end of this*
" *century,* either the parliament will reform itfelf from *within,* or be reformed with
" a vengeance from *without.*" Thus fpoke one of the mafters of the puppet-fhew.
It is beyond the compafs of human language to exprefs the depth of contempt and
deteftation, couched under thefe few words.

On the 28th of February, 1785. Edmund Burke addreffed the Houfe of Commons,
concerning the aftonifhing compofition made with the crediters of the Nabob of Arcot.
In this affair, Mr. Pitt and Mr. Dundas were the principals, and he thus defcribes
their conduct : " Let no man hereafter talk of the decaying energies of nature.
" All the acts and monuments in the records of peculation ; the confolidated cor-
" ruption of ages ; the patterns of exemplary plunder in the heroic times of Roman
" iniquity, never equalled the gigantic corruption of *this fingle act !* Never did Nero,
" in all the infolent prodigality of defpotifm, deal out to his prætorian guards, a
" donation fit to be named with the largefs fhowered down, by the bounty of our
" chancellor of the exchequer (Mr. Pitt,) on the faithful band of his Indian Se-
" poys."

A member in parliament, fome years ago, told Sir John Miller, that he no more
underftood a fubject which he had been fpeaking on, than the animal above mentioned
did the duties of *his* office. This elegant fimilie is to be found in the parliamentary
debates. A note of the date has been miflaid, but the quotation is perfectly
correct.

† Illuftrations of the report, p. 163.

happinefs, which the moft fanguine friend to national improvements can at prefent hardly conjecture. To make this affertion intelligible, and to fhow what benefits may be derived
from the Britifh fifheries, no writer can be cited with more
propriety than John De Witt, Grand Penfioner of Holland.
He informs us, on the authority of Sir Walter Raleigh, that
in the year 1618, the Hollanders employed, on the coaft of
Britain, three thoufand fhips, and fifty thoufand men; and
that for tranfporting and felling the fifh fo taken, and bringing home the returns for them, they required nine thoufand
additional fhips, and one hundred and fifty thoufand men.
Perhaps this eftimate was exaggerated, but the real number of
men and of fhips, engaged in Britifh fifheries, muft have been
very great. De Witt quotes a Dutch writer, who relates, that
in the fpace of three days, in the year 1601, there failed out
of Holland, to the eaftward, between eight and nine hundred
fhips, and fifteen hundred buffes for the herring fifhery. The
Grand Penfioner adds, that from the time of Sir Walter Raleigh, to the year 1667, the Dutch fifheries had been increaf-
ed one third part. He conjectures that the United Provinces
contained two millions and four hundred thoufand people, and
of thefe, that four hundred and fifty thoufand perfons derived
their fubfiftence from the fifheries, and the commerce and manufactures which depended upon them.* Thefe particulars are
here fpecified to prove that Dr. Anderfon has not, on this fubject, made an extravagant fuppofition. He eftimates that one
hundred thoufand fifhermen might find conftant employment
in the Britifh fea. He thinks, that if this number of fifhermen were employed, there would likewife be wanted, twenty
or thirty thoufand mariners for tranfporting the cargoes to
market, and for bringing the neceffary return of falt, of coals,
of grain, of cafks, of the materials for fhip-building, and the
numberlefs articles dependent on an extenfive fifhery.† Suppofing that eighty thoufand of thefe mariners were married, and
that the hufbands had, on an average, four children, the total
amount of their families would be four hundred thoufand perfons. Thefe, added to an hundred and twenty thoufand feamen, would make, in whole, an addition of five hundred
and twenty thoufand Britifh *fubjects*.‡ But this is not all.

* The True Intereft and Political Maxims of Holland, part I. chapters 6 and 9.
tranflated by John Campbell, and printed at London, in 1746. Dr. Anderfon, in his
Evidence before the committee of fifheries, declares, on the authority of De Witt
and others, that in the laft century, two hundred and fixty thoufand perfons were
computed to be employed by Holland in the fifheries alone. I mention thefe different
numbers, without knowing how to reconcile them.

† Evidence before the committee, p. 317.

‡ This word, in its original fenfe, implies fomething that is *caft down* and *trodden
under foot*. When applied in its common acceptation, the choice of expreffion is
happy.

These mariners and their families would not only supply a
great part of the nation with an important article of subsistence,
and thus lessen the wages of labour, but they would afford,
among themselves, a wide market for the commodities of the
farmer and manufacturer. They would thus, in a double way,
promote the public interest. They would lessen the expence
of subsistence, and, at the same time, they would multiply
the excitements to industry. The attainment of these two objects, is the very *Alpha* and *Omega* of national prosperity.
We should then see land, which gives not at present one shilling
per acre of rent, produce from three to six pounds sterling.*
We should see a barren waste of stones and bogs, with scarce a
single blade of grass upon it, converted into luxuriant crops of
wheat and clover. Manufacturing villages would rise in the
wilderness, that is now only distinguished by monumental ves-
tiges of the Picts or the Druids. The farmers and manufacturers would very likely increase to an equal number with that
of the fishermen, and Britain might thus acquire an augmentation of a million and forty thousand inhabitants. The
example of Holland shews that this conjecture is not chimeri-
cal. As the Hebrides and western coasts of Scotland, contain by far the greatest and most important part of this fishery,
they would have a chance of acquiring an addition of seven
hundred thousand people. An hundredth part of the millions
expended upon an ordinary French war, must have been sufficient to found a colony of fishermen in the Hebrides, worth
all our foreign possessions put together. But such a colony
would not have answered the purposes of ministerial corruption. They would not have entangled us in a quarrel with
the rest of Europe. They would not have supplied our rulers
with a plausible pretence for loading the public with extravagant taxes. Mr. Pitt speaks of discharging the national debt,
and of promoting the public prosperity. At the same time he
accepts a Scots revenue of five thousand pounds, that is raised
at an expence of ten thousand. He gives half a guinea per
day to bludgeon-men to drive the electors of John Horne
Tooke from the hustings at Westminster; and an annuity of
five hundred and ninety-five thousand, two hundred pounds
sterling, to the immaculate creditors of the Nabob of Arcot.†

* This has actually happened in Aberdeenshire. The reader may consult an essay
in the Bee. Vol. 7. p. 189.
† The particulars of this edifying transaction are to be found in the works of Edmund Burke, the bosom friend of the " heaven-born minister." A concise account
of it will be given in the Political Progress, Part II. As to the Westminster election,
full information may be had from *Proceedings in an action for debt between the right
honourable Charles James Fox, plaintiff, and John Horne Tooke, Esq. defendant,*
printed in 1792, of which also a summary is inserted in chap. vii. When the
legislature of a country consists of such characters, it is not wonderful that our future
books are crowded with the most atrocious events. As one specimen out of hundreds,
observe what follows.

II

Of ministerial vigilance in collecting the salt duties in the
Scots Highlands, the following particulars will afford a proper
conception. " In these cases, the miscarriage of a letter,
" (and to places where no regular post goes, this must frequent-
" ly happen,) the carelessness of an ignorant ship-master, the
" mistake of a clerk in office, or other circumstances, equally
" trivial, often involve a whole industrious family in ruin.
" There are instances of men being brought to Edinburgh,
" from many hundred miles distance, to the neglect of their
" own affairs, merely because of some neglect or omission of
" some petty clerk in office; which, when rectified, brings
" no other relief, excepting *a permission to return home with*
" *no further load of debt, but the expence of such a journey,*
" *and the loss it has occasioned.* But should the case be other-
" wise, and should the mistake have been committed by the poor
" countryman, though that mistake originated *from ignorance*
" *only,* or was occasioned by the loss of a letter, in going to
" places where no regular posts are established, he becomes
" loaded with additional burdens, which in many cases, all
" his future industry and care will never enable him to dis-
" charge.*

Dr. Smith, in his Inquiry into the Wealth of Nations,
adverts to the Scots herring fishery. He says, that during
eleven years, from 1771, to 1781, inclusive, one hundred
and fifty-five thousand four hundred and sixty three pounds,
eleven shillings sterling of bounties were paid on account of
it. This was, in proportion to the whole quantity of herrings
caught, a premium of twelve shillings and three pence, three
farthings *per* barrel; and this kind of barrels are worth, upon
an average, about a guinea.† Thus the legislature paid four-
sevenths of the market price of a barrel of herrings, as a
bounty to the persons who caught them. Two-thirds of the
buss-caught herrings are exported; and here, a second bounty
is given, of two shillings and eight-pence *per* barrel. The
average number of vessels employed for these eleven years was
about one hundred and ninety-nine. " THREE THOUSAND
" BUSSES have been known to be employed in one year by *the*
" *Dutch* in the (Scots) herring fishery, besides those fitted out

In 1772 a law was made, which declares, " That all persons killing game, on
" any pretence whatever, above an hour before sun-rise, or after sun-set, shall, with-
" out respect to sex or quality, and without any alternative or redemption, be com-
" mitted to prison for three months at least, and be *publicly whipped at noon day,*
" in the town where the prison is situated." Thus, after giving government three
guineas for leave to kill, upon your own ground, a hare that is dear of six-pence, you
are, by this law, subject to be whipped for it, whatever may be your sex or condition. This notable penalty hath since been softened to a fine of five pounds
sterling.

* Illustrations of the report, p. 159.
† Inquiry, Book IV. Chap. 5.

" by the Hamburghers, Bremeners, and other northern ports.[*]"
By the estimate of Sir Walter Raleigh, already cited, a
Dutch bufs carries sixteen hands and two-thirds. If we compute that the veſſels engaged in our fiſhery by foreign nations
amount, all together, to four thouſand, and that each carries
only twelve hands, here are forty-eight thouſand foreign ſailers
reaping the maritime harveſt of Scotland. The bounty firſt
promiſed by parliament for veſſels, was fifty ſhillings *per* ton.
Mr. Guthrie ſays, that " the bounty was withheld *from*
" *year to year*, while, in the mean time, the adventurers were
" not only *ſinking their fortunes*, but alſo borrowing *to the*
" *utmoſt limits of their credit*."[†] It was then reduced to thirty ſhillings. The veſſels are fitted out from the north-weſt
parts of England, the north of Ireland, the ports of Clyde,
" and *the neighbouring iſlands*."[‡] As a complete demonſtration of Dutch good ſenſe, and of our own ſuperlative ſtupidity,
we need only to obſerve that the Hollanders ſend out ten
or fifteen times as many buſſes *without any bounty at all*, as
the Britiſh parliament can collect by a bounty equal to four-
ſevenths of the value of all the herrings taken ; beſides the
remiſſion of ſalt duties, and a ſubſequent bounty on exportation. Mr. Guthrie complains with juſtice, that " this noble
" inſtitution, (viz. the bounty,) ſtill labours under many
" difficulties, from the *caprice* and *ignorance* of the legiſlature."
Thus, an hundred thouſand ſeamen, and perhaps a million of
ſubjects, are loſt to Britain.

A committee of the Houſe of Commons, in one of their
reports, acknowledge, " that the preſent duties upon coals
" are *too high*, and operate more as a prohibition on the uſe
" of the article, *than as a benefit to the revenue.*[§]" The
conſequences of the coal-tax are ſpecified in many paſſages of
the ſtatiſtical account of Scotland. " Perhaps the greateſt
" barrier againſt houſehold induſtry and manufacture among
" us, is *the ſcarcity of fuel* in many parts of the country. A
" human being, pinched with cold, when confined within
" doors, is always an *inactive* being. The day-light during
" winter, is ſpent by many of the women and children in
" gathering *elding*, as they call it ; that is, ſticks, furze, or
" broom, for fuel ; and the evening in warming their ſhivering
" limbs before the ſcanty fire it produces. Could *our legiſlators*
" be conducted through this pariſh, (Kirkenner, in the county
" of Wigton,) in the winter months, could *the lords and*
" *commons*, during the Chriſtmas receſs, viſit the cottages of

* Guthrie's Geographical Grammar. Art. Islands of Scotland.
† Ibid. Art. Scotland.   ‡ Ibid.
§ Appendix to Dr. Anderſon's account of the Hebrides. p. 330.

" the poor through these parts of the *united* kingdoms, where
" nature hath refused coal, and *their* laws have *more than*
" *doubled the price of it*, this would be Shakespeare's *whole-*
" *some physic*, and would, more than any thing else, quicken
" their invention to find ways and means for supplying the
" place of *the worst of laws*."‡ Such legislators ought to be
sent to Bridewell *during the recess*, and to remain there, fed
on bread and water, and without fire or candle, to the end of
the session. Dr. Smith, in his Theory of Moral Sentiments,
remarks, that *the great never consider their inferiors as their fellow*
creatures. The British land-holders illustrate, on all occasions,
the veracity of this maxim. In England, this tax on coals,
when transported by sea, has been very hurtful. "One
" would think," says Lord Kaims, " that it was intended to

---

‡ Statistical Account, vol. iv. p. 147.

The work swarms with complaints on this head. This simple paper appears to
know but little of British lords and commons, when he appeals to their sensibility.
Take notice to what follows :

" A late ball given by Lord Courtney, cost six thousand guineas. He had, among
" other rarities, a thousand peaches at a guinea each, a thousand pottles of cherries at
" five shillings each, a thousand pottles of strawberries at five shillings each, and
" every other article in the same proportion." London Newspapers, 5th May, 1792.
— Another newspaper, some time ago, had this article.

" To such a degree of perfection are dog-kennels now brought, that one lately
" built by Sir William Rowley, at his seat in Suffolk, covers four acres of ground.
" Among other *accommodations for his hounds*, he has erected a warm bath, through
" which each dog is regularly purified, after each day's chase."

Mendoza, the bruiser, some time ago refused to settle the terms of a boxing-match,
until he had consulted his *intimate friend*, the Duke of Hamilton. A letter from him
to this effect, appeared in the public prints. His grace, not long after, invited *his*
friend to a visit at the palace of Hamilton. One day, after dinner, the Duke introduced to his company the subject of boxing. He extolled the talents of the Jew,
and requested leave to bring him in, that the gentlemen present might see the proficiency of his grace in *sparring*. Accordingly, the parties stript, a ring was formed,
and the combat began. The Duke did not strike fair, of which he was repeatedly
warned by his friend. The man was at last so exasperated by his grace per-sling in
foul play, that he gave him a stroke in earnest, which sent the Duke of Hamilton
staggering to the other end of the room. His grace was carried to bed, and the
company dispersed. Mendoza was lately in a Dublin tap-room. His name was discovered,
and he was directly ordered to quit the House. So different are the citizens of Dublin
from this Scots Duke, in *their choice of company.*

The Prince of Wales brought to Newmarket, some time ago, a race-horse of high
reputation. Betts were laid in his favour, but when he came upon the turf, he fell
far behind. He was matched to run a second time next day, and betts were laid
with a very great odds against him. His royal master *accepted the odds*, and betted
to a very large amount in favour of his horse. The whole assemblage of black-legs
considered the Prince as completely *taken in*. But he very soon convinced them that
he was more than a match for the whole gang, at their own weapons. On this second day, his horse resumed his former superiority, and won the race with ease. It
was said, that the Duke of Bedford alone, lost, by this masterly stroke of jockeyship,
twelve thousand pounds sterling. The newspapers estimated *the total balance* in favour of the Prince, from fifty to an hundred thousand pounds. Such was the tri-
umph of

Our eldest hope, divine Iulus.

Late, very late, O may he rule us!

His groom was examined, and, as a swindler, forever exiled from the turf. The
salary of fifty thousand pounds a-year, paid to this hopeful prince, commenced about
the 1st of January, 1781.

" check population.—One may, at the first glance, distinguish
" the coal counties from the rest of England, by the industry
" of the inhabitants, and by plenty of manufacturing towns
" and villages."*

In the year ending on the fifth of January, 1789, the salt
duties for Scotland, produced in whole £ 18043 0 1 1-4
Salaries, incidents, bounties and drawbacks, 8749 9 11 3-4

Net produce of the salt tax - - 9293 10 1 1-2½

Dr. Anderson has just now published a state of the bounties
paid annually by government, upon the Scots fisheries, and
of the premiums, upon the exportation of Scots herrings.‡
They amount, in round numbers, to *twenty-two thousand*
pounds *per annum*. A society in Scotland for encouraging the
fishery, give about *two thousand* pounds. The Scots board of
customs expend about ten thousand pounds annually for cruizers to prevent smuggling; of which sum, the Doctor states
one half, or *five thousand* pounds, to the accompt of salt duties.
Thus, the bounties, premiums, and cruizers cost all together,
twenty-nine thousand pounds a year.‖   The net revenue of
salt for the whole kingdom is about nine thousand pounds.
Thus twenty thousand pounds are sunk. If parliament would
only abolish the tax, and order the Dutch and other foreigners
to stay at home, an hundred thousand mariners, and a million
of subjects might soon be added to the population of Britain.

We have seen the miserable effects of the coal tax. The
Scots duties upon salt and coals together produce hardly a net
eighteen thousand pounds a year to the exchequer.†† At the
same time, the Scots mint, where not even a copper farthing
has been coined for eighty-five years, costs the public annu-
ally - - - - - £ 1000
The keeper of the great seal - - - 3000
The keeper of the privy seal - - - 3000
The lord justice general - - - 2000
The lord register - - - - 1200
The commander in chief of the forces in North-Britain 1460
The vice-admiral - - - - 1000

Carried forward - - - 12660

* Sketches of the History of Man. vol. 1. p. 486. Quarto edition.
† History of the Public Revenue, part III. chap. 6.
‡ This premium, as above stated, is two shillings and eight-pence *per* barrel. Dr.
Anderson has blended under one of these articles, " herrings and hard fish exported
" from England, two thousand pounds." Hard fish had no business in a statement
about herrings; and some deduction from the sum total, should be made on account
of them.
‖ The fame, vol. xi. p. 264.
†† History of the Public Revenue. part III. chap. 6

Brought forward	-	-	-	12660
The knight marifchal	-	-	-	400
The fignet-office is a *direct* tax upon the public, and it				
now nets to the keeper, Mr. Dundas	-			3000
The fafine-office, the fees of which are a fecond direct				
tax, nets to its keeper about two thoufand pounds,				
befides a falary from government, of two hun-				
dred more	-	-	-	-	2200

$$18,260$$

Every one of thefe places is an abfolute finecure, the duties
of which are not difcharged by the perfons who receive the
money. Some of them have nothing to do, but in every one
of them, where bufinefs is really tranfacted, the deputies are
paid over and above, and fometimes very extravagantly, at
the additional expence of the public. The total charge to the
nation, for thefe ten bubbles, extends, as above fpecified, to
eighteen thoufand, two hundred and fixty pounds fterling *per
annum.* Thus hath one part of us been loaded with the plunder of the reft. Thus are fix or eight hundred thoufand Scots
people kept in a ftate of comparative beggary, by the payment
of falt and coal duties, while fix or eight folitary penfioners
riot on the robbery of the poor.

" A *half-ftarved* Highland woman frequently bears more
" than twenty children, while a pampered fine lady is often
" incapable of bearing any.—But *poverty*, though it does not
" prevent the generation, is extremely unfavourable to the
" rearing of children. It is not uncommon, I have been fre-
" quently told, in the Highlands of Scotland, for a mother
" who has born twenty children, not to have *two* alive."[*]
The fum of this paffage is, that multitudes of the children of
Scots Highlanders perifh of hunger, and of the numerous dif-
tempers that follow in its train. The monopoly of land, the
infancy of agriculture, the non-entity of manufactures, with
the accurfed falt excife, and coal duty, form the fountain-head
from whence thefe waters of bitternefs flow.

[*] Smith's Inquiry, book I. chap. 8th.

C H A P. III.

*Reports of the commissioners of public accounts —Crown lands
—Astonishing corn law —British famine in the reign of William Third—Striking picture of Scotch wretchedness at that
period —What Scotland might have been —War in general
—Culloden —The bloody Duke.*

THE practice of granting enormous pensions, has been
carried infinitely farther in England, than on the north
of Tweed. The foil is richer, and the weeds of corruption
grow ranker. As the subject is but imperfectly understood, it
may be worth while to compare the Brobdignag peculators of
London with the Lilliputians of the same kind in this country.
For this end, we may consult a curious and authentic assemblage of evidence published by parliament. During the war
with America, they appointed commissioners to examine the
state of public accounts. The office was performed with fidelity, and the reports published. In the sixth report, we learn,
that the auditor of the exchequer received, in the year 1780,
from his place, a clear profit of   -   £ 14,016   4   1
His first clerk -   -   -   -   -   -   2,752   3   6
The clerk of the pells -   -   -   - 7,397 :2   0 1-2
The four tellers of the exchequer   -   29,267   4   4 1-2
The usher of the exchequer   -   -   4,200

Total to eight persons,   £ 57,833   4   0

The commissioners recommend the abolition of this last office. They observe, that " the chief, if not the only present
" duty of the usher, is to supply the treasury and exchequer
" with stationary and turnery ware, and a variety of other ar-
" ticles, and the exchequer with coals, and to provide work-
" men for certain repairs." In 1780, he provided articles and
repairs to the amount of fourteen thousand, four hundred and
forty pounds, three shillings and six-pence. On the articles,
he was entitled to the very moderate commission of forty *per
cent*; so that the post must, from the first hour of its existence,
have been designed as a job. The net profits were, as above
stated, four thousand guineas. The exact sum pocketed by
the officers and clerks of exchequer, in 1780, clear of all deductions, was seventy-five thousand, eight hundred and sixty-
three pounds, nineteen shillings and three-pence, three farthings, sterling. The report says, that in this year, the *ineffec-
tive* officers of the exchequer, received *forty-five thousand,
three hundred and thirty-two pounds*. This account is too fa-

vourable. We have just seen, that fifty-seven thousand, eight hundred and thirty-three pounds, four shillings, were divided among eight persons. Of these, the only man of business is the first clerk to the auditor, and even he has a salary ten times as large as any merchant would pay to a mere accomptant. The exchequer contains several other clerks with considerable incomes. The four first clerks to the four tellers, received among them, in 1780, five thousand, two hundred and forty-one pounds, and eight-pence three farthings. From this general survey, it may be suspected, that the whole duties of the exchequer might be performed for a tenth part of the wages now paid ; as even, by the present glimmering, we distinctly perceive, that four-fifths of the above seventy-five thousand pounds are absorbed in sinecures. In time of peace, the perquisites would be somewhat less, but the labour would be less in proportion. Fifteen active clerks, at five hundred pounds sterling each, could find, at their own charges, the requisite assistants, and actually perform the business. This simple alteration would, in 1780, have saved to the public, sixty-eight thousand, three hundred pounds. The largeness of *nominal* salaries, forms but the fag-end of the story. After stating various abuses, the report goes on in these words :

" There still remain to be *made up*, the accounts of *four* " treasurers of the navy, to the amount of *fifty-eight millions,* " *nine hundred and forty-four thousand, five hundred and* " *eighty-eight pounds,* and of three paymasters general of the " forces, amounting to four millions, six hundred and sixty- " six thousand, eight hundred and seventy-five pounds, exclu- " sive of the treasurer and paymaster-general in office ; to the " first of whom has been issued, to the 30th of September, " 1780, *sixteen millions, seven hundred and eighty-one thousand,* " *two hundred and seventeen pounds,* and to the latter, to the " end of the same year, *forty-three millions, two hundred and* " *fifty-three thousand, nine hundred and eleven pounds,* and " not one year's account of either is *completed.* So that, of " the money issued to the navy, *seventy-five millions, seven* " *hundred and twenty-five thousand, eight hundred and five* " *pounds,* and of the money issued to the army, *forty-seven* " *millions, nine hundred and twenty thousand, seven hundred* " *and eighty-six pounds ;* together, *one hundred and twenty-* " *three millions, six hundred and forty-six thousand, five hun-* " *dred and ninety-one pounds,* (not including *ten millions, six* " *hundred and forty-seven thousand, one hundred and eighty-* " *eight pounds,* issued to the navy, and *eight millions, one hun-* " *dred and twenty-one thousand pounds,* to the army, to the " end of the last year,) is as yet UNACCOUNTED FOR." These various sums unaccounted for, amount, in the whole, to *one*

hundred and forty-two millions, four hundred and fourteen thousand, seven hundred and seventy-nine pounds. This report is dated the 11th of February, 1782. Lord Holland, paymaster-general of the forces, resigned his office in 1765. He had received near *forty-six millions sterling.* His final account was delivered into the auditor's office, *seven years after his resignation.* Compare this with the prosecution *instantly* raised against a Scots fisherman, for the penalty of a salt bond. The balance actually in the hand of his lordship, when he lost his place, was *four hundred and sixty thousand pounds.* The fourth report says, that upon the 30th of September, 1780, *two hundred and fifty-six thousand pounds* were still due to the public by his representatives, and on a computation of simple interest, at four *per cent. per annum,* that the loss to the nation by the money left in his hands, was, then, *two hundred and forty-eight thousand, three hundred and ninety-four pounds, thirteen shillings, sterling;* as the public have no claim for the interest of money lodged with a paymaster, even *after he is dismissed*.* Thus far the commissioners of public accounts. Now think of the prosecution of a shipwrecked mariner for the duty of six bushels of bonded salt†. It was commonly said that Mr. Richard Rigby, a late paymaster of the forces, cleared annually, seventy thousand pounds from his office, chiefly by keeping in his hands immense sums of public money. What signify the minnows of Tyburn, contrasted with the leviathans of the exchequer, sporting in an ocean of seventeen millions sterling a year? On the waste of public money, Edmund Burke speaks as follows: " It is impossible for a man to
" be an œconomist, under whom various officers, in their se-
" veral departments, may spend even just what they please,
" and often with an emulation of expence, as contributing to
" the importance, if not profit, of their several departments.
" Thus much is certain, that neither the present, nor any
" other first lord of the treasury, has been ever able to take a
" survey, or *to make even a tolerable* GUESS of the expences of
" government for any one year; so as to enable him, with the
" least degree of certainty, or even probability, to bring his
" affairs within compass."‡ And again, " A system of con-
" fusion remains, which is not only alien but *adverse* to all
" œconomy; a system, which is not only prodigal in its *very*
" *essence,* but causes every thing else which belongs to it, to be
" prodigally conducted."‖

---

* These reports are inserted in successive volumes of the New Annual Register. A farther analysis of some of their contents will appear in the second part of this work.

† Supra, chap. 1.

‡ Speech on œconomical reform.   ‖ Ibid.

" In all the great monarchies of Europe, there are still many
" large tracts of land which belong to the crown. They are
" generally forest ; and sometimes forest, where, after travel-
" ling several miles, you will scarce find *a single tree* ; a mere
" waste and lois of country in respect both of produce and po-
" pulation. In every great monarchy of Europe, the sale of
" the crown lands would·produce *a very large sum of money*.—
" The crown lands of Great Britain do not, at present, afford
" *the fourth part* of the rent which could probably be drawn
" from them, if they were the property of private persons."*
This would be a better way to raise money, than by taxing
shopkeepers, pedlars, and servant maids. It has been computed that the crown lands of Britain could be raised in their
value, by setting them on proper leases, or by selling them off
entirely, to a rent of four hundred thousand pounds a year,
more than their present value ; but it would be hazardous to
warrant this vague estimation.

When so great a part of the revenues and resources of a nation are thus miserably cast away, there must be somewhere in
the same political body, a large proportion of distress. Accordingly, Dr. Davenant computes, that twelve hundred thousand
people in England *receive alms*.† Dr. Goldsmith, in his History of Animated Nature, gives a calculation, that in London,
two thousand persons die every year of *hunger*. Dr. Johnson
says, that in 1759, the jails of England contained twenty
thousand prisoners for debt.‡ He conjectures, that five thousand of these debtors perished annually in prison. Dr. Wendeborn states, as a wonted computation, that London contains
forty thousand common prostitutes. It shelters some thousands
of highwaymen, pick-pockets, and swindlers of all kinds, who
gain a regular subsistence by the exercise of their talents.
These are the natural consequence of crown lands lying waste,
and of an hundred and forty-two millions sterling unaccounted
for. In such a condition, we give an hundred and eighty thousand pounds sterling, at a single dash, to pay the debts of a
thoughtless young man. In Holland and Switzerland, beggars, and prisoners for debt, are much less numerous than in
England, because the Dutch and the Swiss are more wise,
more happy, and, to all rational purposes, more *free*, than the
British nation. " There was not, when Mr. Howard visited
" Holland, more than one prisoner for debt in the great city
" of Rotterdam."‖ If half the panegyrics pronounced by

* Inquiry into the nature and causes of the Wealth of Nations. Book v. chap. 2. Part I.

† Sketches of the History of Man. Vol. I. p. 479.

‡ Idler. No. 38. The author adds, in a note, that since first writing, he had found reason to question the calculation.

‖ Burke's speech at Bristol, on the 6th of September, 1780.

Britons upon themfelves are true, genius and virtue can
very feldom be found beyond the limits of this bleffed ifland.
As to civil liberty, an Englifh writer, on that fubject, begins
by fuppofing, that it is confined exclufively to the Britifh dominions.

From thefe mifcellaneous remarks, we proceed to the corn
law, lately paffed. No part of our political fyftem has been
an object of more clamorous applaufe than the bounty granted
by parliament on the exportation of Britifh grain. It is faid
that this bounty was an encouragement effentially requifite for
the intereft of the farmers, becaufe, without it, they would
not venture to raife a fufficient quantity of corn for home confumption. By giving a bounty on exporting it, the farmers
were always certain of a market; and it was fuppofed, that,
but for the profpect of this refource, they would very often
forbear to raife it. The profound policy of this expedient has
been extolled by Lord Kaims, by Sir John Dalrymple, and by
a crowd of other writers, whofe very names would fill a fheet
of paper. Others confider the bounty on exporting corn, as
one of the moft formidable engines of oppreffion, that *the landed intereft* has ever difcharged on the rights of mankind. The
more that the principles of Britifh policy are examined, the
more fhall we, like Rochefter, be convinced, that,

" Dutch prowefs, Danifh wit, and *Britifh Policy*,
" Great NOTHING! mainly tend to thee."

The empires of Japan and China are much better cultivated
than the Britifh Iflands. They know nothing of any fuch
bounty. Ancient Egypt, and likewife Hindoftan, before the
Eaft-India company had deftroyed thirty-fix millions of its
inhabitants, were examples of the fame kind. In thefe countries, and others that might be named, agriculture has advanced
to high perfection; while, at the fame time, the farmers of
England muft be bribed to the plough. There appears an
abfurdity on the very face of this fuppofition; for it is as
reafonable to fay, that the people of Britain cannot, like the
Japanefe, walk without crutches, as that their farmers will
not, like thofe of Japan, raife as much corn as they can,
unlefs they are hired to it by the ftate. Dr. Smith, in his
Inquiry into the Wealth of Nations, hath combated this corn
bounty. Poftlethwaite alfo, in his dictionary, has a paffage
to the fame purpofe; and as the bulk of his book may have
prevented fome people from reading it quite through, we fhall
extract a few remarks on the corn laws.

" There is no complaint more common among our merchants,
" than that foreigners underwork us in almoft every kind of
" manufacture; and can we be furprifed at it? when the gene-
" ral tendency of our laws, is to make labour dear *at home*,

" and cheap *abroad*; when we either forbid our people to
" work, or oblige them to work in the moft difadvantageous
" manner; when we lay all our taxes on trade, or, which is
" ftill worfe for trade, on the *neceffaries of life*; and when we
" contrive to feed the labourers, manufacturers, and feamen
" of foreign countries, with our corn at a cheaper rate *than
" our own people can have it!* To raife the price of corn at
" home, in whatever manner it is done, is the fame thing as
" to lay a tax on the confumption of it; and to do that in
" fuch a manner as leffens the price of it abroad, is to apply
" this tax to the benefit of foreigners."[*] The bounty paid by
law on the exportation of corn, hath, by one account, amounted, in a fingle year, to one hundred and fifty thoufand pounds.[†]
By another account, " the bounty upon corn alone has fome-
" times coft the public in one year, more than *three hundred
" thoufand pounds.*"[‡]

Weekly accounts of the average prices of corn, in different
parts of Britain, are publifhed by authority of parliament.
Before we examine the law fo lately paft on this head, it is
proper to look into thefe weekly reports. We fhal thus learn
upon what fort of information the legiflature went, and how
far they were qualified, by a previous acquaintance with the
ftate of the corn trade, to make laws concerning it.

For the county of Northumberland, there were two returns
of average prices of oat-meal, during the week which ended on
the 28th of April, 1792. A boll weighs an hundred and forty
pounds avoirdupois. At Hexham, in Northumberland, the price
of a boll was faid to be twenty eight fhillings and eight pence.
At Berwick upon Tweed, in the fame county, and at the diftance of no more than fixty miles, the average price, at the
fame time, was only *eleven fhillings and nine-pence.* If thefe accounts of prices were accurate, it would have been an excellent trade to tranfport corn from Berwick to Hexham, where
it would give more than double the fame price. An hundred
pounds employed in this way, muft have returned a clear profit
of an hundred and forty-four and two-fevenths *per cent.* fubtracting only the expence of carriage. The medium is ftruck
between thefe two rates, and twenty fhillings and two-pence
per boll, is returned as the average price of oat-meal, for the
county of Northumberland. No body will believe, or pretend
to believe, that both thefe reports are genuine. It is very likely
that both are untrue. There is a conftant intercourfe between
Hexham and Berwick, and the feveral prices, in every part of
the country, are invariably and univerfally known. To fancy

* Dictionary, vol. 1. p. 560.
† Sketches of the hiftory of Man, vol. I. p. 492.
‡ Smith's Inquiry, Book 4th. chap. 5th.

then such a difference in the rate of corn, is like believing that the water collected behind a dam will keep at its former height, when the dam itself hath been removed. The phyfical abfurdity of the one fuppofition, is not greater than the moral abfurdity of the other. In the fame week, a boll of oat-meal, at *Berwick*, in this very county of Northumberland, is ftated, by the weekly report, at three pounds, two fhillings and fix-pence. Thus, by carrying oat-meal from the one Berwick to the other, a profit might have been gained of more than four hundred *per cent*. The following are the prices in the reports of the fame week, for fome other places. For Weftmoreland, fourteen fhillings and feven-pence ; for Herefordfhire, fifty-fi e fhillings and two-pence ; in Lancafter, fourteen fhillings and eleven-pence ; in Salop, fifty fhillings and eleven-pence ; in Chefter, fifteen fhillings and a penny ; in Bedfordfhire, fifty fhillings and feven-pence. Thefe reports, publifhed by the perfons acting under parliament, are of equal authenticity with Robinfon Crufoe. Yet, as we fhall immediately perceive, the fubfiftence of millions of people may depend on the accuracy of thefe identical weekly reports.*

The new corn law commenced its operations, on the 15th of November, 1791. In every ftage it had received an obftinate oppofition. On one claufe, a committee of the houfe of commons were equally divided, fixty-two on each fide, and the vote of the chairman decided againft it. The act, as now pub-lifhed, fills eighty-four folio pages of confufion and repetition.† By the affiftance of fome gentlemen, I have been enabled to form an analyfis of a part of its contents.

The maritime country of England and Wales, is by this law, divided into twelve diftricts ; and all Scotland into four. To fimplify the difcuffion as much as poffible, let us confine ourfelves at prefent, to the firft of the four diftricts of Scotland. It comprehends the counties of Fife, Kinrofs, Clackmannan, Stirling, Linlithgow, Edinburgh, Hadington, Berwick, Roxburgh, Selkirk, and Peebles. Suppofing that a fcarcity of provifions fhould prevail in the fhire of Edinburgh, wheat, for inftance cannot be imported into it from any other diftrict of Britain, till the average prices of wheat have been afcertained over the eleven counties with which it forms a diftrict. It muft be proved, to the fatisfaction of the fheriff depute of the county, that the average price of wheat is fifty fhillings per quarter ; for, if it is imported, when the price is lower than that fum, there is a duty on the importation, of twenty-four fhillings and three-

* Thefe particulars of the weekly reports were firft publifhed by Dr. Anderfon, in the Bee, vol. IX. p. 9o.
† The remark of Lord Thurlow, above quoted, was perfectly juft. Many an act of parliament, would, as a compofition, *difgrace fchool-boys*.

pence, which is equivalent to a prohibition. But though the public should really be starving, and wheat extravagantly dear, the real price of it can *only* be ascertained to the sheriff depute, by these weekly returns above stated. This is the express injunction of the statute, and these identical returns are of as much actual authority as the croaking of a parrot.

.-ow it must be observed, that in this first Scottish district, fertile and barren counties are injudiciously classed together. Of the eleven above-mentioned, only Fife, Edinburgh and Hadington produce in general good grain. That of the other eight counties is often at the rate of ten or twelve shillings *per* boll, when the grain of Fife, or Edinburgh, sells at eighteen shillings. Put the case then, that the wheat of Edinburgh has risen to fifty shillings, and an importation is wanted from a foreign country. " No," says the sheriff depute of the county. " The grand broker of Westminster elections, viz. *the heaven-* " *born minister*, the jockey peers of Newmarket, with proxies " in their pockets, and the *pocket-list* representatives of St. " Mawes and Old Sarum, have ordered things better. They " have debated and scolded among themselves, upon this sub- " ject, for three months. By two majorities of ten or fifteen " votes out of *eight hundred*, they have produced a *permanent* " corn act, an act of which they boast, as the master-piece of " legislation. *Seven entire statutes* have been repealed to make " room for it. This laconic law has three or four hundred " clauses, which Oedipus could not have explained, and Simo- " nides could not have remembered. By one of these articles, " you are not to import wheat, though you may be starving " for want of it, till the wheat of Peebles and Clackmannan, " has mounted from its present rate of thirty shillings *per* quar- " ter, up to forty. By that time, your own must have risen to " *sixty.* We shall then strike the medium, and suffer you to im- " port it for a duty of half a crown *per* quarter. You need " not grumble. The people of Orkney and Shetland are infi- " nitely worse of. Among them, an ear of corn is an object " of astonishment ; and it is as much inferior in quality to that " of Peebles, as the latter is inferior to yours. You are per- " mitted to import oats when yours rise to seventeen shillings " *per* quarter, for a duty of only one shilling, which goes to " make up the half guinea *per* day to Westminster bludgeon- " men, and the four thousand guineas per annum to the usher " of the exchequer. But when the oats of Orkney, are *nomi-* " *nally* at seventeen shillings, they are in reality dearer than " yours, when at twenty-five or thirty shillings. In a word, you " are graciously permitted to eat bread, perhaps a third part " cheaper, than those beggarly islanders. Mark the superior fe- " licity of your situation ; and let your hearts glow with

" gratitude to the best of princes." The admiring citizens hear their magistrate with silent rapture, and bless their stars that they were born under the British constitution. N. B. His Lordship, notwithstanding his constitutional good nature, had just then endured five or six of them to be shot, in honour of his majesty's birth-day.*—The fallacy of the corn returns has already been mentioned, and we perceive what infinite mischief they may possibly commit. The wheat in the county of Edinburgh may be returned at twenty-five shillings per quarter, when the real price is fifty or sixty, and thus importation may be prevented.

There is another circumstance in this law that deserves attention. The wheat, oats, and barley of England are, in quality, far superior to ours. This is well known to every baker and brewer. At this moment, Edinburgh brewers are buying English barley at eight shillings *per* boll higher than is given for barley of Scots produce, taking the prices of the different counties at a medium. The former is of superior value, by the proportion of fifteen or eighteen to ten.

In Kent, Norfolk, and the other counties of England, subject to this law, the wheat is twenty-five *per cent.* better than that of Scotland. To make the statute equitable, therefore, the people of North-Britain ought to have imported wheat, when it was at forty shillings per quarter, while England should not have been allowed an importation, till English wheat had risen to *fifty* shillings. " This is what a wise and virtuous ministry would " have done and said. This, therefore, is what our ministers " could never think of saying or doing."† English grain, of all kinds, ought to have been raised, for the licence of importation, at twenty or twenty-five *per cent.* higher than Scots grain. The plain meaning of the law is, that the people of Scotland must eat their bread dearer by twenty-five *per cent.* than Englishmen eat theirs. That is the true intent and meaning of this corn law. Every dealer in grain will tell you, on a minute's warning, that he does not understand this statute ; and that he never heard of any body, who could safely undertake to decypher these eighty-four folio pages, about the terms upon which we are to be permitted *to buy our bread.* When the corn merchants of Leith found part of the law totally beyond their comprehension, they applied to the custom-house officers, who frankly declared that they were not able to explain it. In this way a *heaven-born* minister manages the business of a *free* nation.

If a Swifs, or a North-American, were to read this account, he would certainly conclude that Britain is inhabited only by two

* In Charles-street, George's-square. They had been burning an effigy of straw.
† Burke's speech on the creditors of the Nabob of Arcot.

kinds of people, flaves and mad-men. Dr. Anderfon gives a juft idea of this ftatute of defolation. " By the late corn act, it is in " the power of any cuftom-houfe officer ftationed there, (in the " Highlands or Hebrides,) to ftarve nearly half a million of peo- " ple for want of food, almoft *when he pleafes.*" It would re- quire an uncommon degree of penetration, to determine whe- ther the authors of this act are fitteft for bedlam or the Old- Bailey. If the moft inveterate enemies to human happinefs, had confulted for ages together, they could not have devifed a more decifive method, than by this bill, for reducing the labouring part of the Scots nation to the laft extremity of poverty and wretch- ednefs.

With regard to the probable confequences of this corn law, hereafter, we may judge of the future by the paft. " During " fome years previous to the peace of Ryfwick, (which was con- " cluded in 1697,) the price of corn in England was *double*, and " in Scotland *quadruple* its ordinary rate; and in one of thefe " years, it was believed, that in Scotland *eighty thoufand people* " *died of want*."† A tenth part of the expence of one of the Britifh campaigns in Flanders, would have averted from this ifland fo dreadful a calamity. In Aberdeenfhire, the confequences of this famine may ftill be traced. Whole families expired to- gether, and the boundaries of deferted farms were forgotten. To afcertain them is, at this day, fometimes an object of dif- pute. The land bears the marks of the plough; but, having been fo long neglected, has relapfed into its original ftate of barren- nefs; and is now covered with heath, among which may be dif- covered the remains of the dwelling-houfes of the exterminated inhabitants. Thefe extraordinary circumftances have not been obferved by any former writer. They were related to me by Dr. Anderfon, who has an eftate in the county of Aberdeen. We may be perfuaded, that in the other years of this famine, at leaft twenty thoufand additional perfons perifhed of hunger; fo that this reckoning of extirpation amounts altogether to one hundred thoufand lives.

The bleffings that poured upon this country in confequence of the Dutch revolution, afford inceffant exultation in the pages of our hiftorians. The war of 1689, " which *grew out of the re-* " *volution*,"‡ may be termed the firft inftalment of the price of that event. The remedy was like breaking a jaw-bone to remove the tooth-ach. Some authors mention this war with as much tranquility, as if it had begun and ended by the fhooting of a crow. Notice how George Chalmers, efquire, walks on velvet over this fubject. " The infult offered to the fovereignty

---

* Bee, vol. xi. p. 34.
† Memoirs of Great-Britain and Ireland, part iii. book 5.
Ultimate, &c. by mr. Chalmers, p. 107.

" of England, by *giving an asylum* to an abdicated monarch, and
" by disputing the right of a high-minded nation *to regulate its*
" *own affairs*, forced king William into an eight-years war with
" France. Pressed thus by *necessity*, he could not weigh in very
" scrupulous scales the wealth of his subjects, against the su-
" perior **opulence** of his too **potent** rival. Yet animated by his
" characteristic magnanimity, *so worthy of imitation*, and sup-
" ported by the zeal of a people, whose resources were not
" then equal to their ardour and bravery, he engaged in an ar-
" duous dispute, for the most honourable end; the vindication
" of the *independence* of a great kingdom."[*]

On the common principles of hospitality, the king of France
could not have been justified in refusing a refuge to the exiled
king of England. Mr. Chalmers will not say that Lewis should
have delivered up James to William, who was very far from de-
siring so dangerous a captive. But it was wrong, perhaps, to
afford him an asylum? James must have retired somewhere, and,
on the same principles, the English nation might have successively declared war against Spain, Sweden, Denmark, Turkey,
and every other government in the world, where he might be
permitted to reside. It would have been much better for the people of England to behead James at once, than thus meanly to
hunt him around Europe. Britain was not, at that time, in a situation to support a war of eight years against France. The
preceding account of the famine, proves that she was not; and
that the conduct of William, in commencing this quarrel, was
most *unworthy of imitation*. As Mr. Chalmers hath spoke of a
high-minded nation, and the necessity of vindicating its *independence*, which, by the way, the king of France never attempted
to dispute, we may peruse the following account of the condition to which Scotland had been reduced at the termination of
this contest.

"The first thing which I humbly and earnestly propose to **that**
" **honourable court**, (of parliament) is, that they would **take**
" into their consideration, the condition of so many thousands **of**
" our people, who are, at this day, *dying for want of bread*. And
" to persuade them, seriously to apply themselves to so indispen-
" sible a duty, they have all the inducements which **those** most
" powerful emotions of the soul, terror and compassion, can
" produce. Because, from unwholesome food, diseases are so
" multiplied among the poor people, that if some course be not
" taken, this famine may very probably be followed by a plague;
" and then, what man is there, even of those who sit in parlia-
" ment, that can be sure he shall escape? And what man is
" there in this nation, if he have any compassion, who must not

" grudge himself every nice bit, and every delicate morfel he
" puts in his mouth, when he confiders that fo many are alrea-
" dy *dead*, and fo many at that minute *ftruggling with death*, not
" for want of bread, but of *grains*, which I am credibly inform-
" ed, have been eaten by fome families, even during the preced-
" ing years of fcarcity." In another part of this eflay, the writer
informs us, that " there are, at this day, in Scotland, (befides
" a great many poor families, very meanly provided for by the
" church boxes, with others, who, by living upon bad food,
" fall into various difeafes,) *two hundred thoufand people* begging
" from door to door." In a preceding difcourfe, the writer fays,
that there had been " a three-years fcarcity;" fo that in the
whole, this great calamity muft have continued for at leaft four
years, and, perhaps, for a longer time. In 1695, juft as the famine was about its commencement, Mr. Paterfon propofed to
the people of Scotland, his fcheme for founding a colony on the
ifthmus of Darien. " Almoft in an inftant, four hundred thou-
" fand pounds were fubfcribed in Scotland, although it be now
" known, that there was not, at that time, above eight hundred
" thoufand pounds of cafh in the kingdom."† Various obftacles
prevented the firft colony from failing from Leith to the Weft-
Indies, till the 26th of July, 1698. The Scots fquandered about
five hundred thoufand pounds fterling on this fcheme, while
thoufands of their countrymen were dying at home of hunger,
and while two hundred thoufand others were begging from door
to door. This was like a perfon without a fhirt to his back, pretending to bid for a coach and fix. A fwarm of authors agree in
lamenting the deftruction of the Scots colony. They fhould likewife have lamented the folly of our grandfathers in attempting
to found it. Mr. Chalmers may admire, as much as he pleafes,
the *magnanimity* of William, and *a high-minded* nation. Scotland,
with two hundred thoufand beggars fhivering in her bofom, had
very little temptation to interfere in Dutch or Englifh quarrels.
Indeed, this notion of forcing all your neighbours to admit your
title to a crown, is a refinement of modern policy. Caffibellanus
gave himfelf no concern whether Boduognatus, or Vercingen-
torix, acknowledged his claim to the throne of the Trinobantes.

Much noife has been made about the maffacre of Glenco, and
the tragedy of Darien. This famine was a difafter infinitely more
terrible than thefe, yet it has been recorded with far lefs clamorous lamentation. By the greater part of the hiftorians of that period, no notice whatever has been beftowed upon it. Yet, if
William the third, his minifters, and his parliaments, had been
penetrable to human feelings, they would have put an end to

* Second difcourfe on the affairs of Scotland, by Mr. Fletcher of Saltoun,
written in 1698.
† Memoirs of Great-Britain and Ireland, part III. book 6th.

the war, for the fake of putting an end to the famine. They might have done fo on the moft honourable terms. Had William accepted the offers of Louis, " the war of the firft grand " alliance would have ended *four years fooner than it did*, and the " war of the fecond grand alliance might *have been prevented.*"* If any circumftance can add to the folly and the guilt of William, it is this. He was almoft conftantly beaten by Louis in the field; and by the peace itfelf, none of the parties gained one penny of money, or almoft one foot of territory. Yet Sir John Dalrymple, that candid and intelligent hiftorian, has compofed a panegyric on the wifdom and virtues of this monarch. A thoufand other Britifh writers have performed the fame tafk; and the voice of the public hath conftantly fwelled the general chorus of admiration. This is a kind of infatuation and ftupidity, that feems peculiar to the Britifh nation. The French never celebrate the memory of Louis the eleventh, nor did the Roman hiftorians affect to regret the fuffocation of Tiberius Cæfar.

It is remarkable, that though the Scots are perpetually talking of their conftitution, and their liberties, the whole fabric is entirely founded on one of the groffeft and moft indecent acts of ufurpation ever known. I refer to the celebrated Union. The whole negociation bears, on its very face, the ftamp of iniquity. The utmoft care was employed to conceal its infant progrefs from the Scottifh nation, and the bargain was at laft patched up with precipitation by the Scottifh parliament. A fketch of undifputed facts will explain this affertion. The commiffioners for framing the articles were nominated by the queen. Thus two nations refigned a moft important function to this harmlefs but infignificant woman, who, though deftined to a throne, was fcarcely fit for any thing elfe. On the 22d of July, 1706, the articles of union were figned at London, between the commiffioners of the two kingdoms. A refpect for the country required them to be printed, and diftributed, that the people at large, who were to fupport the confequences of this bargin, might, before its ratification, have time to confider of it. A *fealed* copy of the treaty of union was delivered to the Lord Chancellor of Scotland, and its contents were kept fecret, until the 3d of October following, when the Scots parliament affembled at Edinburgh. The articles were then laid before them; and violent debates enfued. If the nation had been capable of acting with unanimity, and firmnefs, proportioned to their feelings, they would immediately have fummoned a convention, elected by the people. They would have declared, that the parliament, by granting leave to the queen, to name commiffioners for Scotland, had betrayed the intereft of their country; and as a tranfaction,

---

* Memoirs of Great-Britain and Ireland, part III. book 10.

founded on fraud, is in itself unlawful and void, they would, if they chose to negociate at all, have begun by throwing aside these articles. Instead of this regular and decisive opposition, the country was filled with tumults, and on the brink of insurrection. At Dumfries, a body of armed men burned the articles publicly at the market cross. The Duke of Athol, at the head of his clan, undertook to secure the pass of Stirling, so as to open the communication between the western and northern highlands. At Edinburgh, the parliament, while deliberating on the treaty, found it requisite to surround themselves with an armed force. This assembly was rent into three different parties; and the agents of the crown began, at length, to despair of obtaining a majority. " The sum of *twenty thousand pounds*, which the queen " privately *lent* to the Scottish treasury,"* contributed to purchase a superiority of votes. Thus the matter went through, and the independence of the Scots nation was bought and sold, with and for its own money. The union was agreed to, " partly," says Mr. Guthrie, " from conviction, and partly through the force " of money, distributed among *the needy nobility*."† When the subject was introduced into the English house of commons, Sir John Packington observed, that this was an union carried on by corruption and bribery within doors, and by force and violence without; that the promoters of it had *basely betrayed their trust*, in giving up their independent constitution; and he left it to the judgment of the house to consider, whether or not men of such principles were fit to be admitted into an English house of commons. It is plain, that the treaty was, in itself, altogether illegal. It exactly resembles the sale of an estate, without the content or knowledge of its owner. The Scotch members of parliament had been authorised, by their constituents, to assemble for the common business of the nation; instead of which, they clandestinely transferred its independence to the best bidder. Edmund Burke, in the speech lately quoted, has a passage that exactly defines it. " A corrupt, private interest," says he, " is set up, in direct opposition to the necessities of the nation. " A diversion is made of millions of the public money from the " public treasury to a private purse." If the parliament of Scotland had a right of transferring its independence to England, we must admit, that the British parliament is equally warranted to form an union with the national assembly of France, in spite of the remonstrances of the people of Britain, and without letting them know the terms of the bargain; and then the two countries may be represented at Paris by forty-five deputies, or, indeed, by one only; for the doctrine of the Scotch salesmen

* Smollet's History of Queen Anne.
† Geographical Grammar, Article SCOTLAND.

amounts to that. If they were warranted in reducing the representatives of the people to forty-five, they had the same right of
reducing them to any lesser number, or, indeed, to cast them
aside entirely. If the parliament of Scotland was entitled to an-
nihilate itself, it had, by the same rule, a power of abolishing
every other part of the government. It could have declared monarchy useless, or, like the commons of Denmark, it could at
once have resigned the liberties of Scotland to the crown. On
the same doctrine, an American congress would be justified for
uniting that continent with Britain; and we may conceive what
their fellow-citizens would think and act on the discovery of
such a conjunction. A detail of the obliquities of this union,
would extend the present chapter beyond its. proper limits. A
full account of it will be given in the course of this work, when
a regular historical narrative commences, beginning with the
year 1688, and ending at the present splendid æra. Without
regard to persons, to parties, or to public opinions, I shall there,
as every where else, hold up truth to the world, as she rises on
my researches, in the naked simplicity of her charms.

After such a review, curiosity may lead us to enquire, if the
Scots government had been honestly conducted, for the last hundred years, what, by this time, *Scotland itself might have been?*
In order to take a proper view of this subject, we must begin by
recollecting, that of one hundred years next after the revolution,
Britain spent forty-two in actual war with other nations of Europe, over and above the campaigns in America, and the quarrels of the East-India company. The following table exhibits,
with tolerable accuracy, the detail of these forty-two years.

Peace.			War.
	1789. May.		8 years 4 months
4 years 8 months	1697. Sept.		
	1702. May.		10 ditto 3 ditto
6 ditto 4 ditto	1712. August.		
	1718. Dec.		2 ditto 6 ditto
5 ditto 8 ditto	1721. June.		
	1727. March.		0 ditto 2 ditto
12 ditto 4 ditto	1727. May.		
	1739. Octo.		8 ditto 7 ditto
7 ditto 0 ditto	1748. May.		
	1755. June.		7 ditto 5 ditto
15 ditto 7 ditto	1762. Nov.		
	1778. June.		4 ditto 9 ditto
6 ditto 2 ditto	1783. March.		
	1789. May.		

57 years 9 months.   42 years.

Frequent armaments have besides taken place, which, though
they did not end in bloodshed, were still very expensive to the

public, and very diftreffing to commerce. Britain has been either fighting, or preparing herfelf to fight, for fixty-five or feventy years out of one hundred. The minds of the people have been kept in a ftate of inceffant fermentation. Their property has been the perpetual fport of ruinous taxes. We never have enjoyed peace for fo long a time together, as was requifite for learning its full advantages. Britain refembles a common bully, who fpends five or fix days of the week on a boxing ftage, and the reft of it, in an excife court or a correction houfe. In fpite of all this folly, the wealth of the country has been continually increafing. " From the reftoration to the revolution, the foreign " trade of England had *doubled* in its amount ; from the peace " of Ryfwick to the demife of king William, it had nearly rifen " *in the fame proportion.* During the firft thirty years of the cur- " rent century, it had again *doubled*" (although three wars, fif- teen campaigns, by land or fea, a Scottifh rebellion, and fix na- val armaments for the Baltic, had intervened). " From the year " 1750 to 1774, notwithftanding the interruption of *an eight-* " *years intervenient war,*" (viz. from 1756 to 1763,) " it ap- " pears to have gained more than *one-fourth*, whether we deter- " mine from the table of tonnage or the value of exports."* We can hardly conceive how very greatly Britifh commerce muft have augmented by this time, if it had not been retarded by thefe abfurd quarrels. As to the taxes, it has been already ob- ferved,† that every fum of money raifed from the public, cofts them ten *percent.* "Never was fo much falfe arithmetic employed, " on any one fubject, as that which has been employed to per- " fuade nations that it is their intereft *to go to war.* Were the " money, which it has coft, to gain, at the clofe of a long war, " a little town, or a little territory, the right to cut wood here, " or to catch fifh there, expended in improving what they al- " ready poffefs, in making roads, opening rivers, building ports, " improving the arts, and finding employment for the poor, it " would render them much ftronger, much wealthier, and " happier. This, I hope, will be our wifdom."‡ The greater part of the money fpent in war, is employed in the purchafe of provifions and military ftores, which are confumed in the courfe of the quarrel, and large fums are always tranfmitted in hard cafh out of this ifland. Thus a capital is transferred from the moft ufeful and beneficent, to the moft favage purpofes. Inftead of building farm-houfes, draining marfhes, and inclofing corn- fields ; inftead of feeding the hungry and clothing the naked ;

* An Eftimate of the Comparative Strength of Britain, by George Chalmers, Efq. p. 46.
† Vide Introduction.
‡ Notes on the ftate of Virginia, by Mr. Jefferfon. Article *Public Revenue* and *Expence.*

inftead of employing the idle, and animating the bufy, of fupporting the induſtry, and embelliſhing the elegance of life, it is deſtined to bribe the brutality of a preſs-gang, or to pamper the rapacity of a contractor, to haſten the difcharge of bombs, the exploſion of mines, and the ſtorming of batteries loaded with grape-ſhot. Transferences of this kind are infinitely numerous, and the concluſion feems evident War is a twc-edged ſword, plunged through the heart of ſociety, and cutting both ways, equally to be avoided for the mifery which it produces, and the happineſs which it prevents. For example, Mr. Burke, fome years ago, afferted in parliament, that fix hundred thouſand pounds per annum were charged for the fupport of the garriſon of Gibraltar, and eighty thouſand pounds for oats, furniſhed to the ſingle legion of colonel Tarleton. Twelve hundred thouſand pounds were charged for the annual proviſions only, of forty thouſand men, and fifty-feven thouſand pounds for prefents to the Indians, for which they had only maſſacred twenty-five women and children.

In feven years, from September, 1774, to September, 1780, incluſive, the number of men raifed for the Britiſh army, was - - - - - - 76,885
            Ditto for the navy   -   -   176,008
                                        ‾‾‾‾‾‾‾
                              Total   252,893[*]

The American war laſted for more than two years after this eſtimate was made, fo that the whole number of men raifed, muſt have been at leaſt three hundred thouſand. Dr. Franklin, in a letter to Mr. Vaughan, fays, that feven hundred Britiſh privateers, whofe crews he calls *gangs of robbers*, were commiſſioned during this war. At an allowance of feventy-two men to each of them, the whole amount was fifty thouſand four hundred. A workman can, upon an average, earn about ten ſhillings a week, which, in London, is at prefent half the common wages of a journeyman taylor. Reduce this to twenty-five pounds *per annum*, and his life may beeſtimated at twelve years purchafe, or three hundred pounds in value to the public. At this rate, the daily labour of the above three hundred and fifty thouſand men, extends to eight millions, feven hundred and fifty thouſand pounds *per annum*. If they had all periſhed in the war, the value of their lives would have amounted, at three hundred pounds *per* head, to one hundred and five millions ſterling. We are farther to obferve, that previous to September, 1774, a very numerous body of men were engaged in the Britiſh army and navy, and thofe perfons are not included in the preceding three hun-

* New Annual Regiſter for 1781. *Principal Occurrences.* p. 40.

dred and fifty thousand. When a corps is raised, and sent out
of the British islands to actual service, it seldom happens that
more than a sixth, a tenth, or a twentieth part of the men, ever
come home again; and even of those who do so, one half are
frequently invalids and pensioners, or beggars. Dr. Johnson, in
his Tour through Scotland, relates, that in the war of 1756, an
Highland regiment, consisting of twelve hundred men, was sent
to North-America, and that of these, only *seventy-six* returned.
Dr. Franklin, in a short essay on war, observes, that privateer
men " are rarely fit for any sober business after a peace, and
" serve only to increase the number of highwaymen and house-
" breakers." From these particulars, we may infer, that at least
three hundred thousand persons were lost to the British nation,
whose lives, in fee-simple, were worth ninety millions sterling.
Of this account, a fifth part may safely be stated as the share of
Scotland; so that the seven tea-duty campaigns, cost an expence
of Scots blood, to the value of eighteen millions sterling. The
war might have been avoided with the greatest facility. In the
historical register of Edinburgh, for the month of December,
1791, there is a curious calculation, founded on the authority
of Sir John Sinclair's statistical reports. By this, it becomes
very probable, that Scotland contains ninety-six thousand fe-
males more than males. It is known, that the number of boys
born exceeds that of girls; and hence this deficiency must be
ascribed to war and emigration. It has been stated above, that
more than six hundred thousand pounds of taxes raised from the
Scots, are fairly carried into the British exchequer; and our absentees at London, who spend the rent of their estates in that
receptacle of profligacy, may be estimated at an additional three
hundred thousand pounds *per annum*. The total sum raised in
Scotland, during the year 1788, by government, was about one
million and ninety-nine thousand pounds. This includes a con-
jectural article of one hundred and thirty thousand pounds as the
duty paid upon goods manufactured in England, taxed there, and
sent down to Scotland for consumption. Of the one million and
ninety-nine thousand pounds sterling, about six hundred and
thirty thousand pounds went in that year into the English exchequer. The remaining four hundred and sixty thousand pounds,
if managed with œconomy, would have been much more than
sufficient for all the purposes of civil government, and the six
hundred thousand guineas might have been saved to the public.
If the union had never existed, the three hundred thousand
pounds *per annum* for absentees, would likewise have remained
in Scotland. If we had enjoyed a wise, virtuous, and *independent*
government, nine hundred thousand pounds a year would have
been retained in this poor, despised, and enslaved country, which
at present goes out of it. Shut up in a remote peninsula, where

nobody comes to moleft us, we, Scotfmen, have no natural bufinefs with Falkland's iflands, or Nootka Sound, with the wilds of Canada, or the fuburbs of Oczakow. The farmers of Fife and Lanerk, are little concerned in the fquabbles between Tippo Saib, and a corporation of Englifh merchants. Shepherds in Galloway fpend their winter evenings without a fire, and weavers of Glafgow go fupperlefs to bed, for the fake of a Dutch frontier, and the balance of ufurpation between German tyrants. For fuch wife ends, we pay fix hundred thoufand guineas a year. We are not fuffered to fifh cod upon our own coafts, but we fight eight or ten years at a ftretch for leave to catch it on the banks of Newfoundland. Since the revolution, Scotland has furnifhed the Britifh army and navy with three or four hundred thoufand recruits, while, at the fame time, England fuffered eighty thoufand of our anceftors to die, in a fingle year, of hunger.

Thefe particulars may affift us in comprehending the deftruction produced to North-Britain by the prefent fyftem of adminiftration. Switzerland is reported, in round numbers, to contain twelve thoufand fquare miles, and two millions of people. The foil is barren, and its furface encumbered with tremendous mountains, yet every acre of land is improved. The beauty of the country, and the felicity of its inhabitants, fill, with rapture, the pages of travellers. North-Britain, and its weftern iflands, exclufive of Orkney and Shetland, form an area of at leaft thirty thoufand fquare miles. The money and the blood expended in foolifh wars, would have converted the whole country, like the Swifs cantons, into gardens, corn-fields and paftures. In proportion to the Helvetic population, we fhould have amounted to five millions, befides another million fupported by the fifheries, and by the manufactures to which they give rife. Inftead of fix millions, the number of people in Scotland does not exceed about fixteen hundred thoufand.

This mournful chapter is now approaching to a conclufion. I fhall only juft remind the reader of the maffacre at Culloden, where Hanoverian ferocity exhibited its utmoft horror. About two thoufand of the miferable rebels were cut to pieces. The wounded were *butchered in cold blood*. The particulars muft be deferred till fome future opportunity. By a very ftrange act of parliament, the duke of Cumberland received, for his fervices, a penfion of twenty-five thoufand pounds fterling, added to fifteen thoufand pounds, which he had before.* The ruffians who performed fuch work, at fix-pence a day, were ftill more execrable than thofe who fet them on. The toad-eating Scots exulted in this tragical confummation of victory. The wretched newfpapers of

---

* This penfion ferved to fwell " *the loaded* COMPOST HEAP *of corrupt influence.*" Vide Mr. Burke's fpeech, as to reforming the civil lift, on the 11th of February 1780.

L

that æra, were crouded with verfes in praife of his royal highnefs. The circumftances of the battle of Culloden itfelf, and the mean and barbarous exultation which it produced, were alike difgraceful to the name of Britain. Cumberland continues to be remembered in Scotland, by the fignificant appellation of *The bloody Duke.*

CHAPTER IV.

Blackstone—His idea of the English conflitution—Default of an hundred and feventy-one millions fterling—Powell—Bembridge—Mary Talbot—Weftminfter election—Anecdotes of the war with America—English Diffenters—Their law-fuit with the corporation of London—Society of friends—Unparalleled oppreffion of that fect in England—Boxing.

THE annals of Scotland prefent us with a feries of frightful maffacres. For any purpofe of moral utility which it can anfwer, the whole narrative had better be forgotten. During the laft forty years, one half of our hiftorians have exhaufted their talents to revile the memory of George Buchanan, by far the greateft literary character that North-Britain ever produced, to decide whether Mary Stuart wrote fome very ftupid letters in French and Latin, and whether Henry Darnley was a cuckold. We fhall certainly find fuperior entertainment in the hiftory of England, which, as her poets and hiftorians tell us, hath always been the native feat of liberty. Here is a fpecimen.

" During the reigns of Charles and James the fecond, above " fixty thoufand Non-conformifts fuffered, of whom *five thoufand* " DIED IN PRISON. On a moderate computation, thefe perfons " were pillaged of *fourteen millions* of property. Such was the " tolerating, liberal, candid fpirit of the church of England."* This eftimate cannot be intended to include Scotland ; for it is likely that here alone, epifcopacy facrificed fixty thoufand victims. Of all forts of follies, the records of the church form the moft outrageous burlefque on the human underftanding. As to Charles the fecond, it is full time that we fhould be fpared from the hereditary infult of a holiday for his baneful reftoration.

At five per cent. of compound intereft, a fum doubles in fourteen years and one hundred and five days, or feven times in a century. Put the cafe, that thefe fourteen millions of property were taken from the English diffenters at once, in 1678, and that they would have doubled eight times between that period, and

* Flower, on the French Conftitution, p. 437. and his authorities.

the prefent year, 1792. This is taking the lofs on the moſt moderate terms. By ſuch an account, the feſt, are, at this day, poorer,
in confequence of thefe perfecutions, than they otherwife would
have been, by the fum of three thoufand, five hundred and eighty-four millions ſterling.

" Our *religious* liberties were fully eſtabliſhed at the reforma-
" tion : but the recovery of our civil and political liberties was a
" work of longer time; they not being thoroughly and completely
" regained till after *the reſtoration of king Charles,* nor fully and
" explicitly acknowledged and defined, till the æra of the *happy*
" revolution. Of a conſtitution fo wifely contrived, fo ſtrongly
" raiſed, and fo highly finiſhed, it is hard to ſpeak with that
" praife, which is juſtly and feverely its due. The thorough and
" attentive contemplation of it will furniſh its beſt panegyric.
" It hath been the endeavour of thefe commentaries, however
" the execution may have fucceeded, to examine its folid foun-
" dations, to mark out its extenfive plan, to explain the ufe and
" diſtribution of its parts, and from the harmonious concurrence
" of thofe feveral parts, to demonſtrate the elegant proportion
" of the whole. We have taken occafion to admire, at every turn,
" the noble monuments of antient ſimplicity, and the more curi-
" ous refinements (falt-bonds, and fo forth,) of modern art. Nor
" have its faults been concealed from view ; for *faults it has*
" (wonderful !), left we ſhould be tempted to think it of more
" than HUMAN STRUCTURE."* The federal conſtitution of
North-America looks, at leaſt upon paper, as well as that of Britain. James Madifon, Efq. of Virginia, is reported to have been
its chief author. The citizens of the united ſtates, or at leaſt a
great majority of their number, regard this conſtitution with
attachment and admiration ; but they never fpeak of Mr. Madifon as a *divinity.* They do not imagine, that fix or eight hundred
years of botching were, as in England, requifite, before a political cub could be licked into any tolerable ſhape ; for two or three
years at the utmoſt, were employed in framing the prefent American conſtitution. In the paſſage now quoted, Sir William Blackſtone has only adopted the ordinary cant of the Engliſh nation.
If any member of congreſs were to fpeak in fuch a ſtrain as to
the legiſlative fyſtem of that country, the whole aſſembly would
confider him as pofitively crazed. As to the " happy revolution,"
the reader may judge from what follows. " Two hundred thou-
" fand pounds a year *beſtowed upon the parliament,* have already
" (1693,) drawn out of the pockets of the fubjects, MORE MONEY,
" than *all our kings fince the conqueſt have had from the nation.* The
" king (William) has about fix ſcore members, whom I can reckon,

---

* Commentaries on the Laws of England, by Sir William Blackſtone. Book IV
chap. XXXIII.

" who are in places, and are thereby so entirely at his devotion,
" that though they have mortal feuds, *when out of the house*, and
" though they are violently of opposite parties, in their notions
" of government, yet they vote as lumpingly as the *lawn sleeves*.
" The house is so *officered* by those who have places and pensions,
" that the king can baffle any bill, quash all grievances, and
" stifle all accompts."* As to the lawn sleeves, the twenty-six fees
of England, are estimated at ninety-two thousand five hundred
pounds, and the twenty-two Irish fees, at seventy-four thousand
pounds, which is in whole, one hundred and sixty-six thousand,
five hundred pounds. On a medium, each of these forty-eight
parsons thus receive three thousand, four hundred and sixty-eight
pounds fifteen shillings sterling *per annum*.

Knowledge, like charity, ought to begin at home. If the British
nation had been thoroughly acquainted with the true character of their own government, they would have saved themselves the trouble of much impertinent encomium upon it, and
of many contemptuous and unprovoked comparisons between
the political situation of their neighbours and themselves. Sir
William Blackstone, and other writers, speak about the *glorious* revolution ; but what *glory* could be annexed to the affair,
it is not easy to see. An infatuated old tyrant was deserted by
all the world, and *fled* from his dominions. His people chose
a successor. This was natural enough, but it had no connection with *glory*. James *ran* away, which precluded all oppor-
tunities for heroism. The character of the leaders in the revolution will not justify a violent encomium on the purity of their
motives. The selection of William was reprobated very soon
after, by themselves, which excludes any pretence to much political foresight. Here then is a *glorious* event, accomplished without an actual effort of courage, of integrity, or of wisdom.
When the Swiss, the Scots, the Americans, the Corsicans, or
the Dutch, wrestled against the superior forces of despotism,
these were scenes of glory, and panegyric becomes intelligible.
But when no resistance happened, the dismissions of a king and
a coachman, were equally remote from it.

One of the principal duties of a national government, is to
take care that the revenues may be duly applied to the service
of the public. But when we look into this branch of administration, the grossest peculation every where meets our enquiries.
Let us take in one hand the commentaries of Blackstone,
and in the other, the reports of the commissioners of public accounts and we shall see how the panegyrist agrees with the accomptant. The tenth report, which is dated the 1st of July,
1783, contains the following, among other curious passages.

* Burgh's Political Disquisitions, vol. 1. p. 450.

"The bufinefs of the auditor of the impreft, to be collected
"from his commiffion, is to audit the accounts of moft of the
"receivers, and of all the officers and perfons entrufted with
"the expenditure of the public revenue.—The accounts which
"at this day remain for the audit of the exchequer, are *feventy
"four millions*, the iffues of twenty one years, for the navy fer-
"vice; *fifty eight millions*, the iffues of eighteen years, for the ar-
"my fervice ; near *thirty nine millions* iffued to fub-accountants;
"together, *one hundred and feventy one millions ;* the receipts and
"iffues of all the provifions for the fupport of the land forces
"in America, and the Weft-Indies, during the late war : all
"thefe accounts muft be paffed. The public have a right and
"good caufe to demand it." Here is an account of *a hundred
and feventy one millions fterling.* that has arrived at the mature
age of *twenty one years*, without a fettlement. The reader may
paufe and ftare, but the report is attefted by five commiffioners,
and publifhed by order of government. There is no great breach
of charity in fufpecting that fifty or fixty millions, out of thefe
one hundred and feventy one millions, have been funk in the
pockets of thofe who handled them. In this report, Mr. John
Powell, acting executor of lord Holland, and cafhier of the pay-
office, makes a principal figure. In 1783, Mr. Powell cut his own
throat. His friend, Mr. Bembridge, accountant of the pay office, had examined and paffed fome accounts between lord Holland and the exchequer. For this fervice, he claimed and received two thoufand fix hundred pounds. It was afterwards found,
that forty eight thoufand feven hundred pounds, chargeable a-
gainft lord Holland, had been improperly concealed, and Bembridge was profecuted for breach of truft. His counfeller, Mr.
Bearcroft, urged a kind of defence, which placed the lawyer and
his client exactly on a level. He faid, that the original blame, if
there was any, refted with the late Mr. Powell, who was the
benefactor of Mr. Bembridge, and that it would have been un-
generous in the latter to have betrayed the former. Lord
North, Mr. Burke, and feveral other birds of the fame feather,
gave Bembridge the higheft character for *integrity.* Lord
Mansfield was of a quite oppofite opinion. The jury found
Bembridge guilty. He was fined in two thoufand fix hundred
pounds, and condemned to fix months of imprifonment. The
author of the new annual regifter, for 1783, fays, that "he bore
"this *very heavy judgment* with great fortitude and compofure."
His *compofure* muft be afcribed to an hardened front. The fine
was but nominal, as he only repaid money which he had not
earned ; and for an intended fraud of forty eight thoufand
pounds, fo trifling a confinement, in which he could enjoy all
the luxuries of life, was no punifhment at all. If Bembridge had
been a poorer man, it is likely that his fentence would have been

very different, at leaft, if we may conjecture from the following cafe. "On the 18th of December, 1790, at the adjourned fef-
"fion of the Old Bailey, Mary Talbot refufed to accept his ma-
"jefty's pardon. She faid, that her return from tranfportation,
"was on account of three dear infants, and that as fhe could not
"take them with her, *fhe had rather die*. The recorder pointed
"out the dreadful precipice on which fhe ftood; as it was moft
"likely, when her refufal was intimated to his majefty, that fhe
"would be ordered for execution. She ftill perfifted, and was
"taken from the bar *in ftrong convulfions*." This article is copi-
ed from a London newfpaper. The original crime, or the fubfequent fate of Mary Talbot, I have not learned. She had moft
likely been tranfported for fome petty theft; and, after endur-
ing the agony of a thoufand deaths, was now to be hanged for
it; while Bembridge efcaped with what was equal to no fentence
at all. A man muft poffefs the apathy of marble, who can read
this parallel without indignation. Scotland, for her humble
fhare in the bleffings of fuch a government, pays fix hundred
thoufand guineas of net cafh *per annum*, tranfported entirely
out of the country; befides her paying very fmartly for foldiers,
tidewaiters, excifemen, and all other forts of conftitutional cater-
pillars. Great and manifold have been the advantages of the union. It was highly worth our while to borrow twenty thoufand
pounds from the treafury of England* to fecure this treaty by
the purchafe of a majority in our incorruptible parliament.
When Horace Walpole difcovered that Scotfmen had more
fenfe than other people, he had certainly been thinking of
this loan, or of the verfes that we publifhed in praife of the
duke of Cumberland, after the battle of Culloden, or of our attempting to found a colony under the equinoctial line, at an
expence of five hundred thoufand pounds fterling, while two
hundred thoufand Scotch men, women, and children, were begging from door to door, and thoufands and ten thoufands of
others were dying of hunger. Perhaps he was alfo reflecting
upon our magnanimous conflagration of a Roman catholic chapel, at Edinburgh, about fifteen years ago, and upon our heroi-
cally raifing a few regiments, after the defeat of Burgoyne, in
1777, to fubfcribe a fecond convention at Saratoga. Or Mr.
Walpole may have been abforbed in admiration at the management of our royal boroughs, where twenty or thirty felf-elected
perfons govern the revenues of the whole community. The city
of Edinburgh, including Leith, has about eighty thoufand inhabitants, and an income that may be gueffed at about fixty, or an
hundred thoufand pounds fterling. This revenue is under the

* Supra Chap. III.
† Catalogue of Royal and noble authors.

absolute management of between thirty and forty self-elected individuals; while the citizens at large, have no more to say in the disposal of this money, than an equal number of Greeks or Jews, in the administration of the revenues of the Grand Turk. Let us proceed with the subject of national expenditure, and illustrate what Blackstone so happily terms *the more curious refinements of modern art.*

Some times, a British minister gives an example of œconomy; for instance, in the case between George Smith, a publican of Westminster, and George Rose, esquire, joint secretary to the treasury, clerk of the parliament, master of the plea office, and representative for the borough of Christ church. Mr. Smith was an agent employed by Mr. Rose, in the contested election for Westminster, between lord Hood, and lord John Townshend. Mr. Smith detected six hundred bad votes, that had been given for lord John Townshend. In this business he was engaged from the 21st of September, 1789, to the 17th of April following, a space of thirty weeks; and Mr. Smith charged for his services, half a guinea per day. The account amounted, at this rate, to one hundred and ten pounds five shillings sterling, or three shillings and eight-pence for each vote. Mr. Smith was a person in decent circumstances; and as this task was neither agreeable, nor even reputable, his demand seems to have been extremely moderate. A great part of the money must have been expended in doing the work. The account, when it first appeared, was stated in these words, *six hundred bad votes, bludgeon men, &c. humbly submitted.* On the 21st of July, 1791, the cause was tried before a special jury, in the court of king's bench, and Rose was cast; so that, this experiment of ministerial frugality was not successful. Smith had been prosecuted in an excise court, and after a suit of three years, condemned in a fine of fifty pounds. Rose interfered, and half of the fine was not paid. This account is extracted from that printed of the trial. As to the defence, Mr. Erskine, counsel for the plaintiff, said, that a more mean, paltry, shabby, contemptible one, he never saw brought into a court of justice. Mr. Rose must hold an elector of Westminster very cheap, if he does not imagine his vote worth three shillings and eight-pence. In a Westminster election, at least, there seems to be nothing of " *more than* " human structure."

The seventh report of the commissioners of public accounts, bears date the 19th day of June, 1782. The subject of it is the expenditure of public money in America, during the last war. " The hire only of waggons, horses, and *drivers,* employed un- " der the management of the quarter-master general, from the " 25th of December, 1776, to the 31st of March, 1780, was " three hundred and thirty eight thousand, four hundred and

" thirty five pounds, eight shillings, and six-pence three far-
" things, exclusive of provisions, forage, repairs, and other con-
" tingent expences." The commissioners next state the actual
price of waggons and horses, and the common rate at which
they were hired. They affirm, that the owner of such a waggon
and horses, received back his purchase-money, *in less than five
months.* " After which, if possessed of fifty large waggons, and
" two hundred horses, (and the waggons and horses were, in ge-
" neral, the property of *a few officers only*,) he will have, as long
" as he can continue them in the service of government, a clear
" income of nine thousand eight hundred and eighty five pounds
" eight shillings and four-pence, a year, *secure from all risk.*"
The hire of the whole waggons and horses employed by the
British troops, was, upon a medium, eighty seven thousand,
nine hundred and fifty-one pounds per annum. " The prime
" cost of the waggons and horses, *at the highest price*, is forty
" four thousand one hundred and fifty pounds. This sum being
" deducted from eighty seven thousand, nine hundred and fifty
" one pounds, leaves the clear profit of *forty three thousand eight
" hundred and one pounds*, for the first year." From the subsequent part of the time, the purchase-money of the horses and
waggons did not fall to be deducted, so that the profits became
exorbitant. In the short period of three years and a quarter, this
statement " gives the sum of two hundred and forty one thou-
" sand, six hundred and ninety pounds, paid by the public, be-
" yond what it would have cost them, had the property of these
" waggons and horses belonged to government." In a word, the
public paid all together, two hundred and eighty five thousand,
seven hundred and forty pounds, for the hire of horses and waggons, when the horses and waggons themselves could have been
purchased for forty four thousand, one hundred and fifty pounds.
The reader will observe, that the incidental expences or damage,
for example, the death of a horse or the breaking of a wheel, were
paid for over and above by the public. A homely comparison
may illustrate this abuse. A tradesman goes into a tap-room,
and calls for a quart of porter, of which the common price is
four pence. He gives the waiter half a crown, and, instead of
drinking the liquor, he throws it into the face of the best customer that has ever entered his shop. Every body would imagine such a man out of his senses. The conduct of the British
parliament justifies the suspicion of the king of Prussia, that they
had certainly been bitten by a mad-dog.* They paid, in the
above instance, about seven times the real price of waggons and
horses for the hire of them, and these, when hired, were employed in traversing the continent of America, in the rear of

* Vide Introduction.

immense bands of highwaymen who were to load them with booty, while the British merchants and manufacturers might have been acquiring millions of guineas, by an amicable and honest intercourse with that very country. Sir William Blackstone says, that a thorough and attentive contemplation of the English constitution, will furnish its best panegyric. This constitution can only be valuable, in the same degree that it is practicable, for, if *it cannot be reduced to practice*, it is of no more use than the republic of Plato, or the Utopia of Sir Thomas More. When we examine it, by the test of experience, we are immediately overwhelmed in an ocean of follies, and of crimes. Nothing can more compleatly prove its extreme imperfection, than the manner in which the British nation is every day bubbled out of its public money. The seventh report, which we are now quoting, forms a striking monument of the gross manner in which we have been cheated. These reports compose one of the most instructive, and useful publications, that ever appeared in any country. They contain mountains of incontestible evidence, that a great part of the constitution, *if we are to judge by the present practice of it*, is absolutely, and irrecoverably rotten; and yet, I have never seen them quoted in any one of the numerous pamphlets that are constantly issuing from the presses of political reformation. I do not recollect to have heard even their existence mentioned by any person whatever; and though they must be perfectly familiar to a few individuals, they are as totally unknown to the great body of the people, as the archives of Memphis. As being of higher authority than the performance of any private remarker can be, they seem proper to be placed in opposition to Sir William Blackstone. We shall, for the present, quit them, with the following particulars.

From the 1st of January, 1776, to the 31st of December, 1781, ten millions, and eighty three thousand, eight hundred and sixty-three pounds, two shillings and six-pence sterling, were transmitted to North-America, for the extraordinary services of the British army, within that period. Of these ten millions, it is to be apprehended, that five or six millions were pilfered on their way to the public service. The commissioners give long details of fraud and imposition.* The following passage is a satisfactory specimen of the stile of their report; at the same time, that it condenses much interesting information.

" Of the ten millions and upwards that have been issued for
" these services to North-America, within the last six years, ac-
" counts of a few officers only, amounting to about eleven hun-
" dred thousand pounds, have been as yet rendered in the pro-
" per office. The accounts of about one hundred and forty
" thousand pounds more are ready; so that the expenditure of

" eight millions, and seven hundred and sixty thousand pounds,
" still remains to be accounted for.

" By an account of the yearly average number of his majesty's
' forces serving at New-York, and its dependencies, from the
" 1st of January, 1776, to the 31st of December, 1780, extracted
" from returns of those forces made to us from the war-office,
" pursuant to our requisition, it appears that the number of the
" forces decreased every year from 1778 ; but, from the ac-
" counts of the contractors for remitting, the issue for the extra-
" ordinary services of that army, greatly encreased during the
" same period.

" In the account of the issues to the officers in the four depart-
" ments, we find that the warrants issued to the quarter-master
" generals, since the 16th of July, 1780, and to the barrack-
" master general since the 29th of June, 1780, and to the com-
" missaries general, since the 25th of May, 1778, have been
" all temporary, for sums on account ; that no final warrant
" has been granted since those several periods. So that these
" sums have been issued, without even the ceremony of a quar-
" terly abstract, and the confidential reliance on the officer, that
" his vouchers are forth coming.

' Of these ten millions, there have been issued to Canada,
" between the 1st of June, 1776, and the 23d of October last,
" two millions, two hundred and thirty six thousand, and twen-
" ty pounds, eleven shillings and seven-pence ; a province,
" whose military operations, since the year 1777, the public
' are not made acquainted with. This issue has been increasing
" every year, and no apparent reason for it ; and upon the ex-
" penditure in this province, there exists no check or controul
" that we know of whatever. These are circumstances of *suspi-
" cion* and *alarm.*"

The following law-suit deserves particular notice, because the
proceedings which give rise to it, were not the actions of a single
individual, but composed a deliberate conspiracy by one great
body of people in England, against the property of another. At
the same time it serves to exhibit " the harmonious concurrence,
" the elegant proportion, and the more curious *refinements* of
" modern art."

In the year 1748, the corporation of London resolved to build
a mansion-house. The scheme required money, and to procure
it, they passed a by-law. They pretended to be anxious for getting *fit* and *able* persons to serve the office of sheriff to the corporation, and they imposed a fine of four hundred pounds and
twenty marks upon every person, who, being nominated by the
lord-mayor, declined to stand the election in the common-
hall. Six hundred pounds were laid upon every person, who,
being elected by the common-hall, refused to serve that office.

The fines thus raised, were appropriated for building the manfion-houfe. In confequence of this law, feveral diffenters were
nominated, and elected to the office of fheriff. By the corporation act, made in the thirteenth year of Charles the fecond, no
perfon could be elected as fheriff, unlefs he had taken the facra-
ment, in the church of England, within a year preceding the
time of his election. If he accepted the office, without this
qualification, he was exprefsly punifhable by the ftatute. If a
diffenter, therefore, had, in virtue of fuch an election, acted as
fheriff, he would have been feverely chaftifed. Hence the gentlemen of that perfuafion refufed the office, and paid their fines, to
the amount of more than fifteen thoufand pounds fterling. One
of the perfons thus elected was blind ; another was bed-ridden.
Thefe were the *fit* and *able* perfons, whom the corporation of
London chofe as fheriffs. The practice went on for feveral years.
This corporation of London had been an affembly of the moft
arrant fharpers, or fuch a project for building a manfion-houfe
never could have entered into their minds. It is impoffible, that
any mortal, poffeffing a fpark of common honefty, fhould have
been concerned in it. At laft Allen Evans, efq. a diffenter, refufed
to pay this fine. An action was brought againft him in the fheriff
court of the corporation of London ; and in September, 1757,
judgment was given againft him. He appealed to the court of
huftings, another city court, and in 1759, the judgment was
affirmed a fecond time. At laft it came before the houfe of lords,
where, on the 4th of February, 1767, it was finally fet afide.
We are not informed whether Mr. Evans paid his own expences.
If he did fo, it might have been cheaper for him to pay the fine.
On this occafion, lord Mansfield pronounced a fpeech. " The de-
" fendant," faid his lordfhip, " was by law incapable, at the time
" of his pretended election : and it is my firm perfuafion that he
" was chofen becaufe *he was incapable.* If he had been capable,
" he had not been chofen : for they did not want him to ferve
" the office. They chofe him, becaufe, without a breach of the
" law, and an ufurpation on the crown, he could not ferve the
" office. They chofe him, that he might fall under the penalty
" of their by-law, *made to ferve a particular purpofe.*—By fuch a
" by-law, the corporation have it in their power, to make every
" diffenter pay a fine of fix hundred pounds, or *any fum they*
" *pleafe ;* for it amounts to that."*

In this fpeech, lord Mansfield expreffes the utmoft deteftation
againft every kind of religious perfecution, as againft natural religion, revealed religion, and found policy. He declares, that he
never read, without rapture, the liberal fentiments of De Thou,

* Letters to the honourable Mr. Juftice Blackftone, by Philip Furneaux, D. D
Appendix, No. 2.

on this fubject. His lordfhip then adds thefe remarkable words. " I am forry that of late, his countrymen (the French,) have be- " gun to open their eyes, fee their error, and *adopt his fentiments.* " I fhould not have *broke my heart,* (I hope I may fay fo, without " breach of *chriftian charity,*) if France had continued to cherifh " the Jefuits, and *to perfecute the hugunots.*" When **Nero** fet fire to Rome, or when Caligula wifhed that the Roman people had on- ly one neck, they might have been partly excufed, as either drunk or mad. Neither of thefe humble apologies can be ad- vanced for lord Mansfield. When the Tartars once conquered China, it was propofed, in a council of war, to extirpate the in- habitants, and turn the country into pafture. As his lordfhip was not a Tartar, nor had any profpect of driving a herd of cat- t'e through France, he ftill remains without an excufe or mo- tive, as to the *cafe in point,* that could lead him to fuch a horrid fentiment. We fhall quit this fubject, with a fhort citation from *The fincere Huron.* " He talked," fays Voltaire, " of the revo- " cation of the edict of Nantes with fo much energy, he deplor- " ed, in fo pathetic a manner, the fate of fifty thoufand fugitive " families, and of fifty thoufand others, *converted by dragoons,* " that the ingenuous Hercules could not refrain from fhedding " tears."

It is foreign to the plan of this work, to enter into a detail of all the outrages which have been committed upon Englifh diffenters; but there is an affertion in a letter publifhed by George Rous, efquire, that cannot be paffed over. Speaking of the late riots at Birmingham, he has thefe words. " Government love an oc- " cafional riot, which, with the affiftance of the military, is eafily " fuppreffed ; in the mean time, it alarms the votaries of a for- " did luxury ; makes them crouch for protection ; and teaches " them patiently to endure evils impofed by the hand of power. " Accordingly, for more than a month, preceding the 14th of " July, all *the daily prints in the intereft of the treafury, laboured to* " *excite a tumult.*" He adds, " to let loofe the rigours of juftice, " might have been a cruel facrifice of *their friends.*" This gen- tleman is a member of the houfe of commons, and of refpecta- ble character and abilities. He thus exprefsly charges the Britifh miniftry with having excited incendiaries to burn the houfes of peaceable citizens. The practice of Mr. Pitt correfponds with the theory of lord Mansfield.

An act of religious toleration and relief is to take place in Scotland, within fix months after the 1ft of July, 1792. It con- tains the following claufe. " If any perfon fhall be prefent twice " in the fame year, at divine fervice, in any epifcopal chapel or " meeting-houfe in Scotland, whereof the paftor or minifter fhall " not pray in exprefs words for his majefty, by name, for his " majefty's heirs or fucceffors, and for all the royal family, in

" the manner herein before directed, every person so present,
" shall, on lawful conviction thereof, for the first offence, forfeit
" the sum of five pounds, sterling money." One half of the fine
goes to the informer, and if the culprit cannot pay, he is to suffer six months of imprisonment. For any future offence, conviction produces two years of imprisonment. In virtue of this
act, it would be very easy for a swindling parson to fleece his flock.
He has only to get his chapel as completely filled as possible, to
place two or three informers in every corner of it, and then, in
his prayers, to forbear all mention of his most sacred majesty. If
four hundred persons were present, this might be converted
into a job of two thousand pounds sterling; as the statute makes
no exceptions in favour of those who should interrupt the person in the midst of the service. The principal actor in the farce,
might, by connivance, abscond; but there is still one difficulty
unprovided for. The informers themselves must have been present at the perpetration of this crime, and therefore they are
equally guilty with the rest of the audience. It ought to be sti-
pulated, that every informer is, in the first place, to receive his
own pardon. The rest of the act is of a piece.

The institution of Sunday-schools, was at first highly popular
in England. The established clergy have since become jealous of
the plan, and Mr. Rous, himself a churchman, gives, in his letter,
some authentic and shameful examples of this fact. The church
of England, in spite of many excellent characters among its
divines, appears to be somewhat lame in its *political* principles.
Its champion, Dr. Tatham, one of the *acting* incendiaries at Birmingham, published a letter some time ago, which has these words.
" It would be a terrible thing, indeed, if all the people of Eng-
" land should learn to read and write." Since the publication
of his letter, Dr. Tatham has received a promotion in one of the
English universities, an article of intelligence that hath been for-
mally announced in the public newspapers. From this circumstance, it appears, that certain members of English universities, instead of wanting to illuminate the minds of the people, are anxious to keep them in the dark. From their approba-
tion of Dr. Tatham, a natural inference is, that we ought all,
as quickly as possible, to forget our alphabet; and consequently, that universities themselves are to become useless. At present
some of their members appear to be much worse than useless,
since they desire to level the rest of their fellow-creatures to the
rank of dogs and horses. We ought to have prevented the citizens of Boston and Philadelphia from learning to read and write.
If they had not been able to read their charters, they hardly
could have discovered the breach of them. Such are the present
principles that guide the internal administration of England.
The houses of dissenters are burnt; and the rabble of the church

are to be prevented from learning to subscribe their names. The baseness and absurdity of our behaviour to foreign nations vanishes in an abyss of domestic infamy.

No man has any business to interfere with the religious opinions of his neighbour. As for a national church, we might as well set up a national laboratory, and oblige every person to buy a periodical quantity of pills. It is just as reasonable to make a man pay for drugs that he will not swallow, as for sermons that he will not hear. If we must have tyrants, ten thousand apothecaries would be less pestiferous than a corporation of ten thousand such vandals as Horseley and Tatham. If every clergyman had, like St. Paul, been a journeyman carpenter, and delivered his sermons without a fee, we should not have heard quite so much of theological butchery. Look into ecclesiastical history, and you will there see, that in consequence of *episcopal* ambition, a thousand pitched battles have been fought, ten thousand cities have sunk in ashes and blood, a million of gibbets have been erected, and an hundred millions of throats cut. From the restoration of Charles the second, to the revolution, a space of twenty eight years, one half of the Scotch nation were hunted like hares and partridges, by bishops and their biped bloodhounds. Englishmen have insulted the rest of mankind, as ignorant of their civil and religious rights. The following narrative will explain the present claim of England to the epithet of a *free* country, and whether it is not, in some degree, as Dr. Johnson says of Jamaica, " a den of tyrants, and a dungeon of " slaves."

On the 3d of July, 1789, the order of the day in the British house of peers, was for the second reading of the bill " for pre- " venting vexatious proceedings with respect to tythes, dues, " or other ecclesiastical, or spiritual profit." Earl Stanhope, who had brought in this bill, moved, that it should be committed. His lordship explained the religious scruples, which prevented quakers from paying tythes. Their scruples were recognized by law. By an act of parliament, in the reign of king William, it was enacted, that tythes due by quakers, might be recovered in a manner different from tythes due by any other persons; providing always, that the sum to be levied, was *under ten pounds*. If the sum was higher, they were still at the mercy of *the church*; so that even this act of protection was very defective. The earl said, that after this *humane* law had past, the common way of recovering tythes from a quaker, was by application to two justices of the peace, who granted a warrant to distress his goods. Of late, some clergymen have not been contented with recovering their tythes, in this way, but have seized and imprisoned the quakers themselves. About two months ago, his lordship said, that a quaker, a man of some property, had been caſt into the common jail of Worceſter ; he was there ſtill, and, though confined for a ſum of only five ſhillings, *muſt remain there for life*.

The act of William is in itſelf imperfect ; but beſides, two methods are known, by which it can be evaded, or ſtrictly ſpeaking, contradicted. In the firſt place, the ſtatute book, that jumble of juridical deformity, contains an unrepealed law, paſt in the reign of Henry the eighth, * which affords full ſcope to eccleſiaſtical vengeance. By this act, which was made above an hundred years before the ſect of quakers exiſted, when any man refuſed to pay his tythe, application was directed to be made to two juſtices of the peace. They " ſhall have power to attach " the perſon againſt whom ſuch requeſt ſhall be made, and com- " mit him to ward, there to remain, without bail or mainprize, " until he ſhall have found ſufficient ſurety, to be bound by re- " cognizance or otherwiſe, to give due obedience to the proceſs, " decrees, and ſentences of the eccleſiaſtical court." Lord Stanhope ſubjoined, that as quakers, by their religion, never can give ſuch obedience, this law is, to all quakers, *impriſonment for life*. By ſeveral other acts, the refuſal to pay tythes, makes the offender ſubject to excommunication in a ſpiritual court, and that again is to be followed by impriſonment. The ſum of the whole was, that the act paſt in the reign of William to protect the quakers, had no real value.

At Coventry, his lordſhip ſtated, that ſix quakers had lately been proſecuted for about four-pence each, as eaſter offerings. The expences of the ſpiritual court, charged againſt them, came to an hundred and ſixty-five pounds, eleven ſhillings ſterling. Their own expences were an hundred and twenty-eight pounds one ſhilling and ſix-pence. Two ſhillings of eaſter offerings were thus to coſt two hundred and ninety-three pounds, twelve ſhillings and ſix-pence of expences. The authors of this proſecution could, by application to two juſtices of the peace, have recovered their two ſhillings, at the charge of perhaps two or three guineas. " As, by their religion, the quakers can never " pay, *nor any of the other quakers for them*, ſome of them have " been excommunicated ; the conſequence of which is, that " they cannot act as executors, that they cannot ſue in any " court, to recover any debt due to them, and in forty days af-

---

* An hundred ſheets of paper would not be large enough to contain the catalogue of his majeſty's crimes. " He was ſincere, open, gallant, liberal, and " capable at leaſt of a temporary friendſhip and attachment." Hiſtory of the houſe of Tudor, by Mr. Hume, chap. vii. He murdered his wife Anne Boleyne, by the verdict of a jury of twenty-ſix Engliſh peers ; a verdict that ſhews what wretches both peers and jurors may ſometimes be. The day after the maſſacre of this unfortunate woman, he married another. In the courſe of his *Reformation*, ninety colleges, and an hundred and ten hoſpitals, for the relief of the poor, were by one act of parliament annihilated.

" ter excommunication, they are liable to be sent to prison,
" there to remain till death shall deliver them from a jail, where
" they may be dying for years, and perish by inches; and this
" merely for *the sake of a few pence*; which few pence even might
" have been immediately recovered by means of the *humane* act
" of king William, *had the priest thought fit*."* It was criminal in
the legislature to leave them at his mercy.

" These," said earl Stanhope, " are instances of ecclesiastical
" tyranny and oppression, and of cold, deliberate, and consum-
" mate cruelty, which would disgrace any set of men whatever."
Some persons at Coventry, who were not of the society of
friends, raised money by subscription, to put a stop to the prosecutions against these six men. But lord Stanhope was of opinion, that the remedy would be dangerous, if not fatal, to the
whole society. This example of humanity would only serve to
whet the avarice of the proctors of the spiritual court. " Every
" quaker in the kingdom," said his lordship, " may, as the law
" now stands, be *imprisoned for life*; and it is the more cruel, for
" persons so imprisoned, are not *admitted to bail*." The bill that
gave rise to these remarks was rejected.

The philosophical ideas of Dr. Tatham have made considerable progress among his countrymen. In Scotland, it is the
bitterest reproach to tell any man that even his grand-father
could not read. In England, the case is sometimes otherwise ;
and the utter destitution of acquaintance with an alphabet, is
visible in the gross manners of some individuals among the ordinary classes. The disgraceful practice of boxing, continues to
be highly popular in England. Thirty, forty, or fifty thousand
pounds are sometimes betted among the spectators, on the pro-
wess of a favourite champion. Ten thousand persons have been
known to travel fifty miles to attend a match of this kind; which
is always accompanied by a variety of inferior battles amongst
the mob. The price for tickets of admission within the pali-
sadoes, is commonly half a guinea ; but they are very frequently
overturned, in the course of the combat, by the tempestuous
curiosity of the rabble. The high roads from London to the
scene of action are, on such occasions, crouded with carriages
and horsemen ; and the inns and ale-houses, for a considerable
distance round the country, are shure of being overwhelmed
with customers. It is usual for the partisans of each combatant
to bring cockades in their pockets ; which, if he gains the victory, are transferred to their hats. The first nobility and gentry
make no scruple to officiate on the stage as umpires, bottle-hol-
ders, and seconds. They commence pupils to the " professors of
" the *science* of pugillism," and are ambitious of being consulted in

* Debrett's parliamentary debates, vol. 26, part second, p. 264.

fettling the terms of a match. One of the various treatifes on this *noble* fubject has been dedicated to Lord Barrymore, with rapturous encomiums on his Lordfhip's proficiency in the art. The antagonifts are ufually knocked down ten, fifteen, or twenty times, before the conteft comes to an end. The printers of newfpapers difpatch emiffaries to the fpot ; and fortunate is he who can obtain, by exprefs, the moft early detail of the particulars of the engagement ; which are transferred into the monthly magazines for the edification of the rifing age.

In Scotland or Ireland, an Englifhman, who behaves properly, may refide, to the end of his life, without hearing a fingle national reproach. But one-half of the inhabitants of England difplay the moft illiberal contempt for the reft of mankind, that ever diftinguifhed a civilized people. "Some years ago," fays Dr. Wendeborn, " fcarcely any body durft fpeak French in the " ftreets of London, or in public places, without running the " rifque of being infulted by the populace, who took any fo- " reign language to be French ; and frequently faluted him, who " fpoke what they did not underftand, with the appellation of " *French dog.*" This practice becomes highly ridiculous, when we reflect that London affords a hofpitable rendezvous to half the fwindlers, quacks, and adventurers in Europe ; nor is there any other nation, which, both abroad and at home, affords fuch numerous and egregious bubbles. On the continent, an Englifh traveller is conftantly marked out by landlords, tradefmen, connoiffeurs, and fiddlers, as a victim of peculiar impofition ; though it is true, that thefe gentry very frequently find themfelves miftaken. In the laft century, England poffeffed a very extenfive commerce in the Levant ; and the polite cuftom above quoted from Dr. Wendeborn, has, very likely, been imported from the ftreets of Conftantinople, the only other metropolis at leaft on the furface of this planet, where it is ufual to addrefs ftrangers with a fimilar falutation.

CHAPTER V.

Civil lift—Accumulation of fifteen millions—Dog kennels—George the firft—His liberal ideas of government—George the fecond—His hofpitality at the burial of his eldeft fon—Excife.

" IT is impoffible to maintain that dignity, which a king of " Great-Britain ought to maintain, with an income in any " degree *lefs*, than what is now eftablifhed by parliament."*

* Commentaries on the Laws of England, by Sir William Blackftone. Book 1. chap. viii.

Sir John Sinclair has given a long account of the civil lift. By this, it appears, that between two and three hundred thousand pounds annually are paid out of it, for *efficient* officers of ftate, ambaffadors and judges, for example. In 1785, the royal family, with its fiddlers, chaplains, wet nurfes, lords of the bed-chamber, rockers, groom of the ftole, and nymphs of the clofe-ftool, a ftation worth forty-eight pounds a year, coft all together, about fix hundred and fixty thoufand pounds fterling. Mr. Burgh fpeaks in the following terms of the civil lift.

" There we find places piled on places, to the height of the
" tower of Babel. There we find a mafter of the houfehold,
" treafurer of the houfehold, comptroller of the houfehold, cof-
" ferer of the houfehold, deputy-cofferer of the houfehold,
" clerks of the houfehold, clerks comptrollers of the houfehold,
" clerks comptrollers deputy-clerks of the houfehold, office-
" keepers, chamber-keepers, neceffary-houfe-keepers, purveyors
" of bread, purveyors of wine, purveyors of fifh, purveyors of
" butter and eggs, purveyors of confectionary, deliverers of
" greens, coffee-women, fpicery-men, fpicery-men's affiftant-
" clerks, ewry-men, ewry-men's affiftant-clerks, kitchen-clerks
" comptrollers, kitchen-clerk-comptroller's firft clerks, kitchen-
" clerk-comptroller's junior clerks, yeomen of the mouth,
" under yeomen of the mouth, grooms, grooms children, paf-
" try-yeomen, harbingers, harbingers' yeomen, keepers of ice-
" houfes, cart-takers, cart-taker's grooms, bell-ringers, cock and
" cryer, table-deckers, water-engine turners, ciftern-cleaners,
" keeper of fire-buckets, and a thoufand or two more of the fame
" kind, which if I were to fet down, I know not who would
" take the trouble of reading them over. Will any man fay, and
" keep his countenance, that one, in one hundred of thefe hang-
" ers-on is of any real ufe? Cannot our good king have a poach-
" ed egg for his fupper, unlefs he keeps a purveyor of eggs, and
" his clerks, and his clerks deputy-clerks, at an expence of five
" hundred pounds a year, while the nation is finking in a bot-
" tomlefs ocean of debt? Again; who are they, the yeomen of
" the mouth, and who are the under-yeomen of the mouth?
" What is their bufinefs? What is it to yeoman a king's mouth?
" What is the neceffity for a cofferer, where there is a treafur-
" er? And, where there is a cofferer, what occafion for a de-
" puty-cofferer? Why a neceffary-houfe keeper? Cannot a king
" have a water-clofet, *and keep the key of it in his own pocket?* And
" my little cock and cryer, what can be his poft? Does he come
" under the king's chamber-window, and call the hour, mi-
" micking the crowing of the cock? This might be of ufe be-
" fore clocks and watches, efpecially repeaters, were invented;
" but feems as fuperfluous now, as the deliverer of greens, the
" coffee-women, fpicery men's affiftant-clerks, the kitchen-

" comptroller's firſt clerks and junior clerks, the grooms' chil-
" dren, the harbinger's yeomen, &c. Does the maintaining ſuch
" a number of idlers ſuit the preſent ſtate of our finances? When
" will frugality be neceſſary, if not now? Queen Anne gave
" an hundred thouſand pounds a year to the public ſervice.*
" We pay debts on the civil liſt of ſix hundred thouſand
" pounds in one article, *without aſking how there comes to be a de-*
" *ficiency.*"†

The following converſations, on the ſame ſubject, betweeen
the late princeſs of Wales and Mr. Dodington, cannot fail to excite the attention and ſurpriſe of every reader. " She," the princeſs, " ſaid, that notwithſtanding what I had mentioned of the
" king's kindneſs to the children, and civility to her, *thoſe things*
" *did not impoſe upon her;* that there were other things which
" ſhe could not get over; ſhe wiſhed the king was leſs civil, and
" that he put leſs of *their* money into his own pocket; that he
" got full thirty thouſand pounds *per annum,* by the poor prince's
" death. If he would but have given them the duchy of Corn-
" wall to have paid his debts, it would have been ſomething.
" Should reſentments be carried beyond the grave? Should the
" innocent ſuffer? Was it becoming ſo great a king *to leave his*
" *ſon's debts unpaid?* and ſuch inconſiderable debts? I aſked her
" what ſhe thought they might amount to? She anſwered, ſhe
" had endeavoured to know, as near as a perſon could properly
" enquire, who, not having it in her power, could not pretend to
" pay them. She thought, that, to the tradeſmen and ſervants,
" they did not amount to ninety thouſand pounds; that there
" was ſome money owing to the earl of Scarborough, and that
" there was, abroad, a debt of about ſeventy thouſand pounds.
" That this hurt her exceedingly, though ſhe did not ſhew it. I
" ſaid, that it was impoſſible to new-make people; the king could
" not now be altered, and that it added much to the prudence
" of her conduct, her taking no notice of it. She ſaid, ſhe could
" not, however, bear it, nor help ſometimes giving the king to
" underſtand her, in the ſtrongeſt and moſt diſagreeable light.
" She had done it more than once, and ſhe would tell me how
" it happened the laſt time. You know, continued ſhe, that the
" crown has a power of reſumption of Carleton houſe and gar-
" dens for a certain ſum. The king had, not long ſince, an in-
" clination to ſee them, and he came to make me a viſit there.
" We walked in the gardens, and he, ſeeming mightily pleaſed
" with them, commended them much, and told me that he was
" extremely glad I had got ſo very pretty a place. I replied, it

* The reader may be acquainted with the progreſs and termination of this
act of royal munificence, by conſulting anecdotes of the earl of Chatham, quarto edition, vol. 11, p. 50.
† Political Diſquiſitions, vol. 11. p. 128.

" was a pretty place, but that the prettiness of a place was an
" objection to it, when one was not sure to keep it. The king
" said, that there was, indeed, a power of redumption in the
" crown, for four thousand pounds, but surely, I could not ima-
" gine that it could ever be made use of against me! How
" could such a thought come into my head? I answered, no;
" it was not that which I was afraid of, but I was afraid, there
" were those who had a better right to it, than either the crown or
" I. He said, oh! no, no, I do not understand that; that cannot be.
" I replied, I did not pretend to understand those things, but I
" was afraid, there were such people. He said, Oh! I know nothing
" of that. : do not understand it; and immediately turned the dis-
" course. I was pleased with the ingenuity of the attack, but
" could not help smiling at the defence, nor she neither, when
" she told it."*

This princess was mother to the present king of England;
and these debts of her husband, the prince of Wales, are still
unpaid. The English laws have declared, that the king can do no
wrong. This maxim justifies George the third for neglecting to
pay the servants and tradesmen of his father. But if a private
person had behaved in the same way, his conduct would have
been regarded as the most shabby, dishonourable, ungrateful,
and even dishonest, that can be imagined. The loss of these
ninety thousand pounds must have injured, or perhaps ruined,
a multitude of families, besides the seventy thousand pounds
owing abroad, which may have reduced some very honest men
to insolvency. At the same time, the king of England has the
command of more ready cash than any man in Europe; and as if
Europe itself, with all its repositories, were not sufficient to contain his wealth, he has lodged large sums in the public funds of
North-America.

" We talked of the king's accumulation of treasure, which
" she reckoned at four millions. I told her, that what was be-
" come of it, how employed, where, and what was left, I did
" not pretend to guess; but that I computed the accumulation
" to be from twelve to fifteen millions. That these things, with-
" in a moderate degree, perhaps less than a fourth part, could
" be proved beyond all possibility of a denial; and, when the case
" should exist, would be published in controversial pamphlets."†
One might suppose this accumulation to be incredible, but the
affair admits of an easy solution. In 1756, Dr. Shebbeare published letters to the people of England. In the third letter, he
says, that " during wars carried on solely for Germanic interests,
" the English have spent in paying and sustaining those powers,

* Dodington's Diary, p. 167.
† Ibid. p. 290.

" *twenty-eight millions*, hiring princes and people to defend their
" own territories, and protect their own properties.—Of this
" fum, *two millions three hundred thousand pounds*, English money,
" *has* been paid to the elector of Hanover, as subsidies for troops
" hired to defend their own country.—Since the blessed acces-
" sion of this family to the throne of these realms, the elector
" of Hanover must have been enabled to save, from his Ger- .
" manic revenues, by not residing on the spot, at least *two hun-*
" *dred thousand pounds* annually. These sums, without entering
" into a strict calculation of encreasing interest, like a Change-
" Alley broker, and yet not rejecting it, must, without doubt,
" have doubled themselves to the amount of *sixteen millions four*
" *hundred thousand pounds.*" Dr. Shebbeare was sent to the pillory,
but that does not affect the force of his facts. Besides all this
money, and his salary as king, George the second extracted
from parliament many very large sums, to the extent of five
hundred thousand pounds at once, as will be fully detailed in
another place. The affertion of Mr. Dodington is, in itself,
extremely probable, and the authenticity of the Diary has been
universally admitted. It is much to be lamented, that a government, formed, as Sir William Blackstone says, upon such *solid
foundations*, was not able to hold America in absolute subjection.
If the contents of this single chapter could have been published
in that country, at the commencement of the late revolution, it
is next to impossible that such a being as an American tory would
have existed. The colonies did not seem to have known one hundredth part of the reasons which they really had for striving to
break our parliamentary handcuffs.

In 1755, Mr. Pitt had a conference with the duke of New-
castle, which has been recorded by Mr. Dodington. A short
specimen may serve to shew how the British nation has been
bubbled by government. " The duke *mumbled* that the Saxon
" and Bavarian subsidies were offered and *pressed,* but there
" was nothing done in them ; that the Hessian was perfected,
" but the Russian was not concluded. Whether the duke meant
" unsigned, or unratified, we cannot tell, but we understand it
" is signed. When his grace dwelt so much upon the king's *ho-*
" *nour*, Mr. Pitt asked him, what, if out of the FIFTEEN MIL-
" LIONS *which the king had saved*, he should give his kinsman of
" Hesse one hundred thousand pounds, and the czarina, one
" hundred and fifty thousand pounds, to be off from these
" bad bargains, and not suffer the suggestions, so dange-
" rous to his own quiet, and the safety of his family, to be
" thrown out, which would, and must be, insisted upon in a
" debate of this nature ? Where would be the harm of it ? The
" duke had nothing to say, but desired they might talk it over
" again with the chancellor. Mr. Pitt replied, he was at their

" command, though *nothing could alter his opinion.*"† Much has been faid about the integrity of Mr. Pitt. It was the extremity of bafenefs in him and others, to keep fuch a fecret. This man has been very lucky, in gaining a popular character. We admire his *integrity*, and the Americans, even at this day, revere his generous exertions in their behalf. He declared loudly, in parliament, that he would not fuffer the colonies *to manufacture a hob-nail for a horfe-fhoe.*

The reader will here obferve, that thirty-feven years have elapfed fince George the fecond had faved FIFTEEN MILLIOMS from the civil lift. It has been faid above, that a fum at five *per cent.* of compound intereft, doubles itfelf in fourteen years and an hundred and five days. Now, at this rate, thefe fifteen millions would, in thirty-feven years, have multiplied to more than ninety-one millions and an half. It is indeed true, as Mr. Dodington fays, that we cannot tell *what has become of it*, or *how it has been employed*, but we know that none of the money has been applied to the national fervice. We have fince paid feveral large arrears into which the civil lift had fallen, and an hundred thoufand pounds *per annum*, have been added to the royal falary. At the fame time, the nation has been borrowing money to pay that falary, the expences of Gibraltar and Canada, for the fupport of the war-fyftem, and other matters, nominally at three or four *per cent.* but in reality, fometimes at five and an half *per cent.* To thefe fifteen millions, we may fafely add a million for the expences of collecting it from the people; and let us again revert to the principle, that a fum taken from their purfes, brings a real lofs of ten *per cent.* At this rate of compound intereft, the fixteen millions would double themfelves once in feven years and fifty-three days, or five times in thirty-feven years and nine months. By this royal manœuvre. the public hath loft five hundred and twelve millions fterling. Thefe fixteen millions, if left in our pockets, would have made the national debt as light as a feather, and all our taxes, a trifling burthen. Great part of the money, if not the whole, was fent to Hanover, and thus utterly loft to Britain.

The princefs dowager of Wales, mother to George the third, once obferved to Mr. Dodington, that " She wifhed " Hanover in the fea, as the caufe of all our misfortunes." Since the year 1714, Britain has been dragged after that electorate, like a man of war in the tow of a bum-boat. Hence the royal accumulation of fifteen millions fterling; and " hence it follows " of neceffity, that vaft numbers of our people are compelled to " feek their livelihood by begging, robbing, ftealing, cheating, " pimping, flattering, fuborning, forfwearing, forging, gaming, " lying, fawning, hectoring, voting, fcribbling, ftar-gazing, poi-

† Dodington's Diary, p. 373.

" foning, whoring, canting, libelling, free-thinking, and the like
" occupations."*

The fum above ftated, might have been employed in clearing,
and planting the wafte lands of Britain and Ireland. In Hamp-
fhire, there is a tract of land, about ten or twelve miles fquare,
all in one body, that ftill lies in a ftate of nature. Salifbury plains
are covered with deer-parks. In an extent of about fixteen miles
long, and five miles broad, we meet with five lodges, where the
deer throng in crouds, and are regularly fed. Thefe particulars
are inferted on the authority of a refpectable gentleman, well
acquainted with that part of England. Other examples of the
fame fort might be given, even in England, though that is by far
the moft populous and beft cultivated part of the three kingdoms.
Many large tracts are ftill fuffered to lie in *commons*, that is, in
natural grafs, which would produce ten times their prefent value
of crops, if properly ploughed and manured. As to Scotland and
Ireland, feven-eighths of the foil is at this moment in a ftate of
nature, not the fmalleft attempt having ever been made for its
improvement. Six miles below Dumfries, and about a mile from
a feat of lord Stormont's, there is an extent of four or five miles
fquare, fometimes covered by the tide, which has broke in upon
it within the laft fifty years. It is furrounded on two fides by dry
land, and could be eafily recovered from Solway Frith. The
fleech is now carried off in large quantities for manure. At the
fame time we are fighting for iflands in the Weft-Indies, like the
dog in the fable, who dropped the *fubftance*, while fnapping at the
fhadow. Befides Salifbury plains, there are numerous deer-parks.
At Goodwood, in Suffex, the duke of Richmond has a park for
game four miles round. The dog-kennel coft ten thoufand

---

* Gulliver's **Travels**, part iv.

To this enumeration may be added *franking*. In 1763, the amount of franked
letters was, one hundred and feventy thoufand, feven hundred pounds. Blackftone's Commentaries, book 1. chap. 8. At that time, the two houfes of parliament
contained, perhaps, feven hundred and fifty members, for Englifh peers were lefs
numerous then than they are now. At a medium, this fum was equal to an annuity of two hundred and twenty-feven pounds, twelve fhillings fterling for each
member. Some commoners paid the wages of their footmen with franks, at half
a crown *per* dozen. About fixteen years ago, Sir Robert Herries, a banker in
London, obtained a feat as member for the five Scots boroughs, included in the
diftrict of Dumfries. His object was faid to be, the faving of poftage on all letters
directed to his office. This was computed at feven hundred pounds fterling a year.
Mr. Pitt has made fome very proper regulations on this head. He was warmly
oppofed by Edmund Burke.

In the Hebrides, four places excepted, no poft-office is eftablifhed. " A letter
" from Skye to Lewis, the direct diftance but a few leagues, if fent by poft, muft
" travel about *twelve hundred miles*, before it can reach the place of its deftination."
Dr. Anderfon's Introduction, p. 28. One is at a lofs to conceive, on what account
the Scots, during the American war affumed, in general, fuch a rancorous antipathy to the caufe of the United States. Their zeal for the Englifh government was
violent; yet as juftly might an ox feel attachment to the farmer who fattens him
for the market.

pounds. There are twenty game-keepers. Before the revolution
in France, above a thousand partridge eggs were brought every
year, from that country. The importation is now stopt. At present, his grace keeps only forty pair of hounds at Goodwood.
Some years ago, it was mentioned in the newspapers, that the
duke of Bedford, for the purpose of hunting, had purchased, and
brought over from France, some hundreds of live foxes. He is,
at this time, building at Wooburn, a dog-kennel; the expence
of which is computed at about *seventy thousand pounds sterling*. If
England contains only an hundred such parks as that of Goodwood,
an hundred square miles of land are lost to the public. Like the
rocks at fort William, and the wilds of Aberdeenshire, every foot
of this land might be converted into gardens and corn-fields. If
we assign an hundred and sixty people to every square mile,
which is less than the reputed population of Switzerland, we
have an extrusion of sixteen thousand persons from subsistence,
for the sake of hares, foxes and partridges. But this is not all.
The duke of Richmond keeps twenty game-keepers, and forty
pair of hounds. His dog-kennel is totally eclipsed by that of
Wooburn; and hence we may reasonably presume, that the
hounds and game-keepers of the duke of Bedford, are still more
numerous. But let us once more take the duke of Richmond
for a standard, and say, that the whole kingdom of England
contains only an hundred times more than his private hunting
establishment. We have then two thousand game-keepers, and
four thousand pair of hounds to raise the price of provisions.
This is a great deal; and yet, it is more likely that the country
maintains twenty thousand pair of hounds than four thousand. The loss of one hundred square miles of land, and
the burden of such a multitude of useless men and dogs, call
loudly for the final destruction of every deer park in Britain.
On the 4th of February, 1791, a petition was presented to the
house of commons from Aulcester, for a tax upon dogs. The
petition states, that " where many dogs are kept, and packs of
" hounds, by gentlemen, the prices of many articles of life are
" so much encreased, (particularly sheep's heads, and other in-
" ferior pieces of butcher's meat, which formerly made an es-
" sential part of the maintenance of the poor,) as to be vastly
" *beyond their reach*, and are now sold only for the *kennels* of their
" opulent neighbours."* The master of a dog-kennel, who sup-
ports it by starving the poor, as completely deserves the gallows
as a horse-stealer or a highway-man. In Scotland also, land-
holders can be pointed out, who squander considerable portions
of wholesome food upon their four-footed vermin. These facts
shew the prodigious waste of land and people, in consequence

* Senator, vol. 1, p. 266.

of the prefent tyrannical fyftem of game laws. Even to the cultivated parts of England, great damage is frequently done in the courfe of a fox-chace. If, to thefe confiderations, we add the many thoufands of horfes that are kept by the rich for hunting, racing, and other trifling amufements, it will turn out that fome hundred thoufands of additional people could be maintained by the food caft away upon fuperfluous quadrupeds. Some writers have dreamed that Britain is overftocked with people. In fact, this ifland could, with Chinefe management, readily fupport quadruple its prefent number of inhabitants. The fame remark applies to almoft every other part of Europe, Holland and Switzerland excepted. While fo many millions of Britifh acres lie uncultivated, we pay fix or feven hundred thoufand pounds a year to the family of a fingle man. At a round calculation, let us guefs, that fifty pounds fterling are fufficient for converting an acre of barren bogs, or moors, into meadows or corn-fields. The fum of fix hundred and fixty thoufand pounds, paid in 1785, to the immediate ufe of the crown, might thus have fertilized an hundred and twelve thoufand acres.

The moft miferable part of the ftory ftill remains to be told; but the particulars muft be deferred to fome future time. The civil lift is a gulf yawning to abforb the whole property of the Britifh empire. We look back without fatisfaction, and forward without hope.

Lord Chefterfield informs us, that George the firft was exceedingly hurt, even by the weak oppofition which he met with in parliament, on account of fubfidies. He complained to his moft intimate friends, that he had come over to England to be *a begging king*. His vexation was, that he could not command money without the farce of afking it; for, in his reign, as at prefent, the debates of parliament were but a farce. Such were the liberal fentiments of the firft fovereign of the proteftant fucceffion.

This king detefted his fon, George the fecond, as an offspring of illicit love. His jealoufy was fatal to the life of count Koningfmarck, a Swedifh nobleman. On the fame account, his wife, the heirefs to the duchy of Zell, died in prifon, after a confinement of thirty-fix years. George the firft fhould have confidered this accident, if real, as a *renovation*, rather than a *corruption*, of the royal blood. For tradition reports, that *his own* mother, the princefs Sophia, bore a refemblance to Elizabeth, maiden queen of England. Like that illuftrious and admired fovereign, Sophia, by the formidable number of her male favourites, attefted the ardor of her fenfibility, and the robuftnefs of her conftitution.

The quarrel between George the fecond, and his fon Frederick, prince of Wales, father to George the third, arofe from a

O

different cause. It lasted for more than twenty years, and will be explained in my succeeding history of the reign of George the second. It was carried to a dreadful height. When old queen Caroline was dying, Frederick requested permission to see her. His mother refused access to her son, and expired without an interview. Fifteen years after, Frederick himself died, and Dodington has obliged us with some anecdotes of his burial. By these we learn, that George grudged a dinner to the courtiers who attended it. The following is part of the account which Dodington gives of this affair.

" At seven o'clock, I went, according to the order, to the " house of lords. The many slights that the poor remains of a " much loved friend and master had met with, and who was " now preparing the last trouble he could give his enemies, sunk " me so low, that for the first hour, I was incapable of making " any observation.

" The procession began, and (except the lords appointed to " hold the pall, and attend the chief mourner, and those of his " own domestics) when the attendants were called in their ranks, " there was not one English lord, not one bishop, and only one " Irish lord, two sons of dukes, one baron's son, and two privy " counsellors," (of whom the author was *one*) " out of these great " bodies, to make a show of duty to a prince so great in rank and " expectation. While we were in the house of lords, it rained " very hard, as it has done *all the season ;* when we came into " Palace-Yard, the way to the Abbey was lined with soldiers, but " the managers had not afforded the smallest covering over our " heads ; but by good fortune, while we were from under cover, " it held up. We went in at the south-east door, and turned short " into Henry the seventh's chapel. The service was performed " without either anthem or organ. So ended this sad day.——There " was not the attention to order the green-cloth to provide them a " bit of bread, and these gentlemen," (the bed-chamber of the late prince,) " of the first rank and distinction, in discharging of their " last sad duty to a loved and loving master, were forced to be- " speak *a great cold dinner from a common tavern in the neighbourhood.* " At three o'clock, indeed, they vouchsafed to think of a dinner, " and ordered one ; but *the disgrace was compleat.* The tavern-din- " ner was paid for, and given to the poor. N. B. The duke of " Somerset was chief mourner, notwithstanding the flourishing " state of the royal family.*"

Judge Page, of *hanging* memory, when once pronouncing sentence of death upon a prisoner, added, by way of consolation, " You have A PITIFUL KING sirrah ! A PITIFUL KING, INDEED !"

In this chapter we have seen a few memorable specimens of

* Dodington's Diary, Dublin edition, p. 72.

the mode in which public money is expended. We shall conclude with some remarks on the method by which it is raised.

"The rigour and *arbitrary* proceedings of excise laws, seem "hardly compatible with the temper of a free nation. For the "frauds that might be committed in this branch of the revenue, "unless a strict watch is kept, make it necessary, wherever it is "established, to give the officers a power of entering and sear- "ching the houses of such as deal in exciseable commodities, at "any hour of the day; and, in many cases, of the night like- "wise. And the proceedings, in case of transgressions, are so "summary and sudden, that a man may be convicted in two "days time, in the penalty of many thousand pounds, by two "commissioners or justices of the peace; to the total exclusion "of *the trial by jury*, and disregard of *the common law*.*" About seven millions sterling, or two-fifths of the whole annual revenues of Britain, are raised by an excise. They are raised in an *arbitrary* manner, and in "disregard of *the common law*." After such an acknowledgment, it seems trifling in this author to cant so much about English liberty. He says, that "from its first original to "the present time, its very name *(excise)* has been odious to "the people of England." If this be true, and if the people are as free as they pretend to be, they might, surely, in the course of an hundred and forty-nine years,† have cast it aside, and placed a better system in its stead. The writer gives a very long cata- logue of commodities that have been excised, and adds these words: "A list, which no friend to his country would wish to "see farther encreased." Since his time, the list has been much enlarged. Excise has always been paid, and always execrated; which shews the folly of the trite aphorism, that an Englishman can only be taxed by *his own consent*, and tried by *a jury of his peers*. As two justices of the peace can supersede the existence of *the common law*, and the right of *trial by jury*, let us enquire what kind of persons they are. In Scotland, we all know, that they are sometimes the most insolent, the most brutal, unintel- ligent and worthless characters in the county where they re- side. The chief qualifications required by the statute of the fifth year of George the second is, that they shall have an hundred pounds per annum clear of all deductions. Blackstone speaks of this affair, in the following terms. "Few care to undertake, and "fewer *understand* the office. The country is *greatly obliged* to "any worthy magistrate, that, without sinister views of his own, "will engage in this troublesome service." (Thus we must com- mence mendicants for people to suspend *the common law*.) "And

* Commentaries by Sir William Blackstone, book 1. chap. 8.
† Excise was first imposed in England, in 1643.

" therefore, if *a well-meaning juftice* makes any *undefigned flip* in
" his practice, great lenity and indulgence are fhewn him in the
" courts of law ; and there are many ftatutes made to protect
" him in the *upright* difchatge of his office ; which, among
" other privileges, prohibit fuch juftices from being fued for any
" OVERSIGHT, *without notice before hand ;* and ftop all fuits be-
" gun, on tender made of *fufficient amends*."‡ Who is to decide
what compenfation fhould be fatisfactory ? This quotation,
when ftript of the verbage that furrounds it, tells us plainly, that
juftices of the peace are very often incapable of executing their
duty, and that *many ftatutes* have been exprefsly framed, to fhield
them from the punifhment deferved by their ignorance. A ma-
giftrate who underftands his bufinefs, needs no peculiar protection. In fhort, we fee, that when a juftice of the peace blun-
ders, the door againft redrefs is both fhut and bolted. The author, indeed, fubjoins, that a juftice, when convicted of *wilful*
or *malicious* injury, is fubjected " to double cofts." But fince it
is next to impoffible to convict or even to profecute him, the latter ftipulation is a mere ftalking horfe. Thefe magiftrates are
removeable at the pleafure of the crown ; a reafon, perhaps,
why they have been chofen as inftruments for fufpending the
ufe of *the common law.*

The morals of the Britifh nation have been degraded by ex-
ceffive taxes. On the 16th of June, 1789, the houfe of commons refolved itfelf into a committee, on the bill for an excife
on tobacco. A few notes from Debrett's parliamentary debates
on that bill, will demonftrate the maturity to which fmuggling
and its twin-fifter perjury, muft have extended. Mr. Pitt faid,
" that at leaft one-half of the tobacco, confumed in the king-
" dom (Britain) was *fmuggled*." The importation of tobacco
" amounted to nearly fixteen millions of pounds, but to four-
" teen *at leaft*. The actual legal importation, he declared, had
" been, on the average, eftimated at *feven millions*." The duty
on each million of pounds, was fixty thoufand pounds fterling ;
fo that if only five millions of pounds were annually fmuggled
into Britain, the revenue was defrauded of three hundred thoufand pounds fterling, and *the fair trader*, if fuch a character can
have exifted, was robbed of his cuftomers and his profits. Mr. Pitt
faid, that previous to the commutation act, which reduced the
duty on tea, about the fame quantity of that article had been
imported, and a very great proportion of it had been fmuggled.
He had made fome regulations for leffening the duty on wines
imported, and from thirteen thoufand tons, the former vifible
importation, it had mounted up to twenty-two thoufand tons.
The additional nine thoufand had formerly been fmuggled. It

‡ Commentaries, book 1, chap. 9.

is no wonder that *a custom-house oath* has long been synonimous
to perjury. The tobacco bill, consisting of an hundred and thirty-five folio pages, past, after long and angry debates. Next year,
an attempt was made to repeal it, and on the 16th of April,
1790, Mr. Sheridan, in a speech on that question, told the following story to the house of commons. An eminent distiller,
of a very fair character, had occasion to dispute a judgment by
which a quantity of spirits had been seized and condemned as
above proof. He maintained that they were not above proof;
that Clarke's hydrometer, by which they had been proved, was
faulty; and that if the spirits were tried by hydrometers accu-
rately made, they would be found to be such as the law required
them to be, and consequently not seizable. The case went to
trial, and turned out precisely as the distiller had stated it to be;
Mr. Clarke admitted that his hydrometer was faulty, and requested that the commissioners of excise would give him leave to
amend and correct it. But, instead of listening to a request so
reasonable and just, they procured a clause to be inserted in a
hotch-potch bill, by which it was enacted that Clarke's hydrometer should, in future, be the legal standard for trying the
strength of spirits.

This hydrometer was acknowledged, by its maker, to be faulty;
and yet the commissioners, so far from granting him leave to
amend it, applied to parliament for an act which sanctioned error, and legalized falsehood and oppression.* Thus far Mr. Sheridan.

CHAPTER VI.

*Edward I.—Edward III.—Henry V.—Ireland—Conduct of
Britain in various quarters of the world—Otaheite—Guin-a—
North-America—The Jersey prison ship—Bengal—General esti-
mate of destruction in the East-Indies.*

AT home Englishmen admire liberty, but abroad they have
always been harsh masters. Edward the first conquered
Wales and Scotland, and, at the distance of five hundred years,
his name is yet remembered in both countries with traditionary
horror. His annals are blasted by an excess of infamy, uncommon
even in the ruffian catalogue of English kings. David Hume,
Sir William Blackstone, and Sir John Sinclair, have celebrated
the talents and atchievements of this detestable barbarian. " The
" English *Justinian* was one of the wisest and most fortunate

* Debrett's Parliamentary Debates, vol. xxvii. page 408.

" princes, that ever fat upon the thone of England. In him were
" united, the prudence and forefight of the ſtateſman and legiſ-
" lator, with the valour and magnanimous ſpirit of the hero."[*]
Edward made war in Paleſtine and in France. He butchered ſome
hundred thouſands of the Welſh and the Scots. He was conſtantly
at variance with his own ſubjects, and exerted every petty fraud
to ſtrip them of their property. The ſpoil thus obtained, was expended with equal criminality. We ſhudder to think of a domeſtic murder; but when a crowned robber, whoſe underſtanding
is perhaps unequal to the office of a poſt-boy, ſends an hundred
thouſand brave men into the field, to deſolate provinces, and hew
nations down like oxen, we call it *Glory*. Thus common ſenſe
and humanity are obliterated by a rhapſody of words. If Edward
the firſt, as a private man, had murdered a ſingle Scot or Welſh-
man, the world would have agreed in thinking that he deſerved
the gallows. But when he *only*, upon the moſt hateful pretences,
butchered three or four hundred thouſand people, we are ſum-
moned, at the end of five centuries, to admire " his wiſdom, his
" good fortune, his valour and magnanimity." As to his *wiſdom*,
it is hard to ſay what England gained by his victories. The Welſh
were independent or thereabouts, in the reign of Henry the
fourth, an hundred years after the death of Edward, ſo that the
merit of finally ſubduing them is to be placed ſomewhere elſe. The
Scots revolted in the life-time of this Edward. He died on a journey to Scotland, for the ſacred purpoſe of extirpating the Scots
nation. He would have been much wiſer if he had ſtaid at home
at firſt, and ſaved himſelf the trouble of an impracticable conqueſt. As to the domeſtic legiſlation of this *Juſtinian*, he hanged
two hundred and eighty Jews in one day. " Above fifteen thou-
" ſand were plundered of all their wealth, and baniſhed the king-
" dom."[†] The ſame writer ſays, that theſe enormities were committed under various *pretences*. "The year thirteen hundred forms
" the diſgraceful epoch of the original debaſement of our ſtan-
" dard coin, when our *Engliſh Juſtinian*, Edward firſt, defrau-
" ded every creditor of eight-pence half-penny in every twenty-
" ſhillings."[‡] An excellent legiſlator he was, to be ſure, when
he cheated the public creditors, and forged bad money. Edward
firſt introduced tonnage and poundage, duties on imports and
exports. He was, in every reſpect, a ſcourge to the human race.

Edward the ſecond wanted to live at peace. Sir John Sinclair
tells us, that his reign is remarkable for " the *inconſiderable* taxes
" levied." He was fond of the ſociety of ſome companions, and
all the hiſtorians mention this mark of good nature, as a very
groſs weakneſs, if not *a poſitive crime*. The heart of a wolf was,

* Hiſtory of the Public Revenue, part 1. chap. 6.
† Ibid.
‡ Eſtimate, &c. by Mr. Chalmers, p. 80.

at that time, an essential qualification, for a king of England. After various rebellions against him, Edward was taken prisoner by his wife. He expired in Berkley castle, by a species of death, too horrible to be described. His real guilt was a social and peaceable disposition.

"The reign of Edward the third is, without doubt, the most " *splendid* in the English history.—His queen pawned her jewels."[*] The king pawned *his crown ;* and this pledge lay unredeemed for eight years. He conquered a great part of France, without any sort of justice on his side. The rapacity of his son, the BLACK prince, as he has been emphatically termed, drove the French into rebellion, and the English out of the country. This conquest, and subsequent expulsion, first planted the seeds of that brutal antipathy to the French people, by which England has been too much distinguished.

> Ferox Britannus viribus antehac,
> Gallifque femper cladibus imminens.
>
> BUCHANAN.

" The Briton, formerly ferocious in his strength, and always " menacing calamities to France." Englishmen pretend to be proud of the horrid ravages committed in that country, by Edward the third, by his son, and by Henry the fifth. The *justice* of their claims has long been given up ; and yet we are deafened about their *virtues*. Englishmen prattle on *French* perfidy, and of sucking in, with their mother's milk, an honest hatred for that greatest of nations. In the French wars of Edward the third, and Henry the fifth, England was plainly the aggressor ; and the country, so far from feeling pride in their victories, ought, if possible, to suppress *that* part of its ancient history. Philip de Comines places the affair in a proper light. He ascribes the civil wars of York and Lancaster, that succeeded the death of Henry the fifth, to the indignation of divine justice. The murder, by Richard the third, of his two nephews, was a diminutive crime, contrasted with the atrocity of Crecy, of Azincourt, and Poictiers. Henry the fifth was a two-fold usurper. " When he " thought," says Horace Walpole, that he had any title to *the* " *crown of England*, the other followed of course." Since his time, the kings of England have called themselves *kings of France*, just like a person advertising that his grand-father had stolen a horse.

Henry butchered numbers of the Lollards, a premature tribe of protestants. The Scots, in great bodies, joined the French, and gave him some checks. On this he pretended, that they were *his* lawful subjects, and hanged those whom he took prisoners, for having *rebelled*. Mr. Hume has employed a long paragraph upon *the character* of Henry. He begins, by saying, that

* History of the Public Revenue, part 1. chap. 6.

" this prince poffeffed *many eminent virtues.*" Henry committed
more mifchief than all the felons ever executed at Tyburn. Yet,
Mr. Hume draws a plaufible picture of him, and fixes a ftrong
impreffion of refpect and kindnefs. Hiftorians abound with thefe
fophiftical portraits. The reader is taught to admire, when
there is room for nothing but execration. Thus are his morals
corrupted, and his underftanding turned topfy-turvy. This is
the moft ufual effect of perufing hiftory. If Henry had only put
to death a fingle Lollard, he certainly could not poffefs *many
eminent virtues.* A mite, in a cruft of cheefe, projecting an or-
rery, would be a lefs extravagant idea than that of a human being defining the nature, effence, and intentions of the Deity.
But, when this phrenzy breaks out into perfonal violence, as in
the cafe of the Lollards, and the quakers at Coventry, the mad-
nefs of the fcheme is forgot in its extreme wickednefs.*

Ireland has long prefented a ftriking monument of the wifdom,
juftice, and humanity of the Englifh nation. That devoted ifland
was, in the end of the twelfth century, over-run by a fet of bandit-
ti, under Henry the fecond. This eftablifhed a divine right. Sir
John Davis informs us, that even in times of peace, it was ad-
judged no felony to kill *a mere Irifhman.* This acquifition proved
very troublefome to the conquerors. " The ufual revenue of Ire-
" land," fays Mr. Hume, " amounted only to fixthoufand pounds
" a year. The queen, (Elizabeth,) though with much repining,
" commonly added twenty thoufand pounds more, which the re-
" mitted from England." The *fupremacy* was, at beft, a lofing
bargain. In war, affairs were, of courfe, an hundred times worfe.
Sir John Sinclair fays, that the rebellion of Tyrone, which lafted
for eight years, coft four hundred thoufand pounds *per annum.*
In 1599, fix hundred thoufand pounds were fpent in fix months;
and Sir Robert Cecil affirmed, that in ten years, Ireland coft England three millions, and four hundred thoufand pounds fterling.
This profufion of treafure was expended in fupporting the piratical conqueft of a country, which did not yield a fhilling of
profit to England, nor pay, even in time of peace, a fourth-part
of the expence of its goverment. The confolation of inflicting
the deepeft and moft univerfal wretchednefs, was the total recom-
penfe afforded to the good people of England. Sir William Petty,
in his Political Anatomy, fays, that in the year 1641, Ireland contained   1,466,000 inhabitants.
He adds, that in 1652, they had funk to   850,000†

Decreafe   616,000

---

* The Englifh nation might, at this day, have been four times more numerous, a thoufand times more happy, and by millions of degrees lefs criminal, if
two-thirds of them had belonged to the fociety of Friends.

† Thefe particulars are borrowed from a quarto edition of Guthrie's Grammar, printed at Dublin. I have not yet feen a copy of the Political Anatomy.

Thus, in eleven years, the Irish nation lost six hundred and six-teen thousand people. In 1641 they had been driven into rebellion, by the tyranny of that English parliament which conducted Charles Stuart to the scaffold. On the incorruptible virtues of that upright band, much nonsense hath been said and sung. By a single vote, they confiscated two millions and five hundred thousand acres of ground in Ireland. The whole island was transformed into an immense slaughter-house. Ireland, governed by an English *republic*, might have looked towards Morocco, as a terrestrial paradise. Compared with the tremendous mass of misery produced by Strafford, Cromwell, Ireton, and the *virtuous* duke of Ormond, the dungeons of the Bastile, or the proscriptions of a Roman triumvirate, shrink into forgetfulness.†

Neither the restoration of Charles the second, nor the *glorious* revolution, afforded much relief to Ireland. The people continued to groan under the most oppressive and absurd despotism, till, in defiance of all consequences, the immortal Swift, like another Ajax,

> Broke the dark phalanx, and let in the light.

He taught his country to understand her importance. At last she resolved to assert it, and, as a necessary arrangement, she arose in arms. England saw the hazard of contending with a brave, an injured, and an indignant nation. The fabric of tyranny trembled to its base ; and it is to be hoped, that a short time will extinguish every vestige of a supremacy, dishonourable and pernicious to both nations. As matters now stand, an Irishman, who loves his country, must be strongly tempted to wish that England were sunk five thousand fathoms below the German ocean. If the rest of Europe has not been reduced to the same distress with Ireland, it is owing to want of power, and not of inclination, on the side of England. The greater part of her wars, commenced against foreign nations, have wanted even a pretence of justice. For instance, in 1652, the immaculate English commonwealth forced the Dutch into a rupture. Mr. Hume assigns the following reasons for it. " Many of the members thought " that a foreign war would serve as a pretence for *continuing* " *the same parliament,* and delaying the new model of a repre- " sentative, with which the nation had so long been flattered. " To divert the attention of the public from domestic quarrels, " towards foreign transactions, seemed, in the present disposi- " tions of men's minds, to be *good policy.* The parliamentary " leaders hoped *to gain many rich prizes from the Dutch,* and to " *distress and sink their flourishing commerce.*" The Romans began the third Punic war for the very same kind of reasons. Blake

P

† Consult a Review of the Civil Wars in Ireland, by Dr. Curry. An epitome of his valuable book, will form a future part of the Political Progress.

was the hero of this conteſt; and it has been cuſtomary to celebrate his virtues. He had exactly the ſame proportion of honeſty
with any other admiral of Corſairs. Plunder and bloodſhed were
the object of his maſters; and if it be true, that he deſpiſed
money, this only ſhews that he was willing to rob and murther
without any farther gratification than that which he ſelt from
the pleaſure of the performance. The Dutch did all that was
poſſible to prevent the war, both before and after a firſt battle
had been fought. The Engliſh behaved with the moſt intolerable
arrogance. This alſo is *an admitted fact*; ſo that the whole guilt
of the quarrel reſted on the ſide of England, even by the ſtate-
ment of Britiſh hiſtorians. Eight bloody and deſperate conflicts
were fought. One of them laſted for two days, and a ſecond for
three. Many thouſands of lives were loſt. Sixteen hundred merchant veſſels were taken from the Dutch, and their fiſheries were
totally ſuſpended. The war laſted for about two years.

Viſit the royal infirmary of Edinburgh, and, along with a
dozen ſtudents, who are half ſmothering a laugh at the agonies
of the patient, contemplate the amputation or the fracture of a
limb. You may then attempt to form a conception of three hundred thouſand ſuch operations, and reflect that *this is war*.

In 1655, Cromwell attacked the dominions of Spain, without
pretending to have received any offence. The two nations had
lived in profound peace for about thirty years. " Several ſea officers," ſays Mr. Hume, " having entertained ſcruples of con-
" ſcience, with regard to *the juſtice of the Spaniſh war*, threw up
" their commiſſions, and retired. No commands, they thought,
" of their ſuperiors, could juſtify a war, which was contrary to
" the principles of *natural equity*, and which the civil magiſtrate
" *had no right to order*." The names of theſe officers ought to be
tranſmitted to poſterity on braſs and marble. " Individuals, they
" maintained, in reſigning to the public their natural liberty,
" could beſtow on it only what they themſelves were poſſeſſed of,
" *a right of performing lawful actions*, and could inveſt it with no
" authority of commanding *what is contrary to the decrees of heaven*."
All this is moſt unqueſtionably true, but obſerve how Mr. Hume
gets over this difficulty. " Such maxims, though THEY SEEM
" REASONABLE, are perhaps too perfect for human nature; and
" muſt be regarded as one effect, though of the moſt *innocent* and
" even *honourable* kind, of that ſpirit, partly *fanatical*, partly re-
" publican, which predominated in England." Thus, when a man
refuſes, at command of government, to commit what he thinks
murder and piracy, he is *partly fanatical*, and his ſcruples, though
they ſeem reaſonable, are perhaps *too perfect for human nature*. A
book that dictates ſuch maxims of depravity is more peſtiferous
to the human heart than the ſophiſms of Hobbes and Machiavel,
or the impurities of Rocheſter and of Cleland. Let us proceed

with our narrative. In the West-Indies, Penn, father to the founder of Philadelphia, and Venables conquered Jamaica; and the crown of Britain continues to hold that island by the same right which a highwayman has to the watch in your pocket. A fleet of Spanish galleons were attacked. Two of them were taken, and the plunder was valued at two millions of pieces of eight. Two other galleons were set on fire. The wife and daughter of the viceroy of Peru were destroyed in the flames, while the distracted husband and father, who might have escaped death, chose to perish with his family.* " The next action against " the Spaniards was more *honourable*, though less *profitable*, to the " nation. Thus we learn from Mr. Hume, that there is a degree of *honour* in burning ships, when you cannot get them plundered, and in destroying innocent passengers, with their wives and children. This *next action*, which was so extremely *honourable*, consisted in the conflagration of sixteen Spanish ships, with all their treasures. " This was the *last* and *greatest* action of the gallant " Blake. Disinterested, generous, liberal; ambitious only of *true* " *glory* dreadful only to his avowed enemies, he forms one of the " most *perfect* characters of the age, and the least stained with " those errors and violences, which were then so predominant. " The protector ordered him a pompous funeral at the public " charge; but the tears of his countrymen were the most honour- " able panegyric on his memory." Mr. Hume should likewise have told us, that Charles the second, caused Blake to be *dug up again*. He himself admits, that the invasion of the Spanish West-Indies " was an *unwarrantable* violation of treaty." Where, then, is the distinction between Cromwell and Barbarossa? There is, surely, none at all. England paid dearly for this war. The property of her merchants in Spain was confiscated to an immense amount; and it was computed that fifteen hundred English vessels were, in a few years, captured by the enemy. These losses counterbalanced the *millions of pieces of eight*, acquired by the perpetration of such horrid crimes.

On the 22d of February, 1665, Charles the second declared war against Holland. When an exile and a beggar, he had been received with kindness in that country; and the general partiality of the people in his favour, had afforded some offence to the late republic of England. His majesty now hasted to discharge his obligations. The motives to this rupture, corresponded with those which led to the former war with Holland, viz. the love of pillage and of slaughter. " The Dutch, who, by industry and " frugality, were enabled to undersell them (the English) in every " market, retained possession of the most lucrative branches of " commerce; and the English merchants had the mortification

---

* He preferred death to a capitulation with tyrants.

" to find, that all attempts to extend their trade, were still turned,
" by the vigilance of their rivals, to their loss and dishonour.
" Their indignation encreased, when they considered *the superior*
" *naval power* of England ; the bravery of her officers and sea-
" men ; her favourable situation which enabled her to intercept
" the whole Dutch commerce. By the prospect of these advan-
" tages, they were strongly prompted, from motives *less just than*
" *political*, to make war upon the states ; and, at once, *to ravish*
" *from them, by force*, what they could not obtain, or could ob-
" tain but slowly, by superior skill and industry." In this passage, Mr. Hume implies, that England acted with *some degree*
both of *policy* and of *justice*. As to the latter, it is evident, from his
own account, that there was not a single spark of it, and as to
the *policy*, the sequel shewed, that it was entirely mistaken. The
English minister at the Hague, presented to the states " a list of
" those depredations, of which the English complained. It is re-
" markable, that all the pretended depredations preceded the
" year 1662, when a treaty of league and alliance had been re-
" newed with the Dutch, and these complaints were then thought
" either so *ill-grounded*, or so *frivolous*, that they had not been
" mentioned in the treaty." Two ships had been claimed by
the English. The matter was referred to a court of law ; and
the states had consigned a sum of money, in case the question
should be decided against them. The matter was still in depen-
dence. The states had offered thirty thousand pounds to the
owners of one of these two ships, in full of their demands, and
the people had resolved to accept of it. They were prevented by
the English ambassador, who told them, that the claim was *a*
matter of state. The whole English nation were violently bent on
a war. " The parliament granted a supply, the largest, by far,
" that had ever been given to a king of England ; *yet scarcely*
" *sufficient for the present undertaking.*" The Dutch "tried every art
" of negociation, before *they would come to extremities*." The war
began. The king of Denmark made, at the same time, an offen-
sive alliance with England against Holland, and another with
Holland against England. He adhered to the treaty with Holland, and seized and confiscated all the English ships in his har-
bours. England could not obtain a single ally, except the insig-
nificant bishop of Munster. One of the naval battles in this war
lasted for four days, and the fleets were finally parted by a mist.
In a subsequent engagement, the English were victorious, and
burnt in the road of Vlie, an hundred and forty merchantmen,
with a large village on the neighbouring coast. The Dutch, in
return, sailed up the river Medway, took Sheerness, destroyed a
number of men of war, insulted Plymouth, Portsmouth, and
Harwich, and sailed up the Thames as far as Tilbury. On the
10th of July, 1667, a peace was concluded upon equal terms.

The war cost the Dutch about three millions sterling, but they were not vanquished. On the 13th of January, 1668, Charles entered into a strict alliance with them. Not long after it was signed, Clifford, a confidential minister of Charles, said *we must have a second war with Holland.* On the 17th of March, 1672, war was actually declared by Charles against that republic. " A " ground of quarrel," says Mr. Hume, " was sought by means " of a yacht, dispatched for lady Temple. The captain sailed " through the Dutch fleet, which lay on their own coasts ; and " he had orders to make them strike, to fire on them, and to per-" severe till *they should return his fire.*" The Dutch admiral came on board of the yacht, and in friendly and sensible terms, repre-sented the absurdity of such conduct. The captain of the yacht did not chuse to continue his fire ; and, for this breach of or-ders, he was, on his return home, committed to the tower. Some other pretences are enumerated by Mr. Hume, and they were all equally ridiculous. A series of dreadful engagements were again fought at sea ; and it does not appear that England gained a single victory. But as France now assisted Charles, the Dutch were overwhelmed rather than vanquished. A peace was signed in February 1674, and the advantages gained by Eng-land were extremely trifling.

These three wars with Holland, and the fourth with Spain, were begun and ended in the short period of twenty-two years. No sober man will attempt to deny that, in every one of them, England was an unprovoked, a perfidious, and a barbarous ag-gressor ; and that she discovered in each of them, an insatiable thirst of piracy and murther. Her conduct both before and since that period hath been exactly of the same complexion ; nor is it likely that she will forbear to insult and rob other nations, till, in the maturity of divine justice, a second Duke of Normandy, shall extinguish her political existence.

In the East and West-Indies, the conduct of the " united " kingdoms" may be candidly compared with the *trial* of Atahu-alpa.

Our sublime politicians exult in the victory of Seringapatam,* and the butchery of the subjects of a prince, at the distance of six thousand leagues from Britain. Yet it would be an event the most auspicious both for Bengal and for ourselves, if Cornwallis, with all his myrmidons, could be at once driven out of India.

But what quarter of the globe has not been convulsed by our ambition, our avarice, and our baseness ? The tribes of the Pa-cific Ocean are polluted by the most loathsome of diseases. On the shores of Africa, we bribe whole nations by drunkenness, to robbery and murder ; while, in the face of earth and heaven,

* On the 6th of February, 1792.

our fenators affembled to fanctify the practice. Our brandy has brutalized or extirpated the aborigines of the weftern continent ; and we have hired by thoufands, the furvivors, to the talk of bloodfhed. On an impartial examination, it will be found, that the guilt and infamy of this practice, exceed, by a confiderable degree, that of any other fpecies of crimes recorded in hiftory. It is far worfe than even the piracies of the Algerines, or the African flave trade ; becaufe, though the two latter have coft millions of lives, yet plunder, not affaffination, is the ultimate object of purfuit ; whereas, a plan, for exciting the Indians to extirpate the people of the United States, holds out no temptation, either of conqueft or of fpoil ; and can arife only from a genuine monarchical and parliamentary thirft for the blood of republicans.

Our North-American colonies, including the Thirteen United States, formed a pretence for long and bloody wars and for an expenditure of two hundred and eighty millions fterling.* We ftill retain Canada, at an immenfe annual charge, that fhall be hereafter fpecified. The money is wrefted from us by an excife, which revels in the deftruction of manufactures, and the beggary of ten thoufand honeft families. From the province itfelf, we never raifed, nor hope to raife, a fhilling of effective revenue ; and the chief reafon why its inhabitants endure our dominion for a month longer, is to fecure the money that we fpend among them. The Britifh commiffioners of public accounts, in their fifteenth report, ftate the following particulars. The amount of cuftoms for 1784, in the ports of Quebec, of Halifax, of Newfoundland, and St. John's, was five hundred and fixty-three pounds fterling ; the expences of collection and incidents, one thoufand, two hundred and eighty-eight pounds. The charges thus exceeded the income by *feven hundred and twenty-five pounds.* This is a fummary of their detail. There feems to have been a miftake, perhaps by the printer, in cafting up the figures, to the extent of fifty-feven pounds. This trifling circumftance is only mentioned to ward off a charge of mif-qnotation.

The mode of conducting our war againft America, correfponded with the juftice of our caufe. At the burning of Fairfield, in Connecticut, " a fucking infant was plundered of part of its " cloathing, while the bayonet was prefented to the breaft of its " mother.† At Connecticut Farms, in the ftate of New-York, Mrs. Caldwell, the wife of a prefbyterian clergyman, was fhot dead, by a mufket, levelled at *her*, through the window of a room, in which fhe was fitting with her children. Permiffion was granted to remove her body, and then the houfe itfelf was reduced to afhes.‡ We have at leaft five or ten thoufand authen-

* Hiftory of the Public Revenue, part III. chap. 2.
† Ramfay's Hiftory of the American Revolution, vol. II. chap. 17.
‡ Ibid. chap. 22.

tic anecdotes of the same kind. The Jersey, a British prison-
ship, at New-York, will be long remembered in the United
States. It is affirmed, on as good evidence as the nature of the
subject will admit, that, during the last six years of the war,
eleven thousand American prisoners died of hunger, and every
sort of bad treatment, aboard of that single vessel. For some time
after the war ended, heaps of their bones lay whitening in the
sun, on the shores of Long-Island. When the illustrious commander at West-Point deserted to Clinton, nothing could be
more *becoming the service*, than his instant promotion to the rank
of a British brigadier-general. Philips, and other British officers,
at once adopted, as their associate and their confidant, this pro-
digy of Connecticut. England is fond of comparing herself to
antient Rome; and, in perfidy and barbarity, she has been a
most successful imitator. But she has neither exerted the inflexible intrepidity, the profound wisdom, nor the dignified pride of
a primitive Roman. Fabius or Marcellus durst not have promoted a Numidian deserter to the command of a legion; nor would
such a person have been suffered, like Arnold, to challenge and
fight a senator for the exercise of his duty.

The peninsula within the Ganges, is the grand scene, where
the genius of British *supremacy* displays its meridian splendour.
Culloden, Glencoe, and Darien, the British famine of four years,
Burgoyne's tomahawks, Tarleton's quarters, the Jersey prison-
ship, and the extirpation of six hundred and sixteen thousand
Irish men, women and children, dwindle from a comparison.

" The civil wars, to which our violent desire of creating na-
" bobs gave rise, were attended with tragical events. Bengal
" was depopulated by every species of public distress. In the
" space of *six* years, half the great cities of this opulent king-
" dom were rendered desolate; the most fertile fields in the
" world lay waste; and FIVE MILLIONS of harmless and indus-
" trious people were either expelled or destroyed. Want of
" foresight became more fatal than innate barbarism; and men
" found themselves wading through *blood* and *ruin*, when their
" only object was *spoil*." This book was published in 1772."
The author, a Scots officer, returned to India *after its publication*.
His return to Bengal proves that the accusation here advanced
was of *notorious* authenticity, and that colonel Dow was prepared
to support it, at the point of his sword.

On the 5th of June, 1792, Mr. Francis said, in the house of
commons, that the Bengal newspapers were perpetually full of
advertisements, for the sale of lands, seized *for want of due payment of revenue*. He held in his hand two of these advertisements;
the one announced the sale of *seventeen* villages, and the other, a
sale of *forty-two*. John Bonnar may, perhaps, live to advertise

* Dow's History of Hindostan, vol. III. p. 79.

Falkir or Muffeburgh for the arrears of a malt-excife. Mr. Francis quoted fome minutes of lord Cornwallis to the fame effect. One of thefe, dated the 18th of September, 1789, was in thefe remarkable words. " I can fafely affirm, that *one-third* of the " company's territory in Hindoftan, is now A JUNGLE, INHABI- " TED BY WILD BEASTS."

In 1785, the Britifh Eaft-India company governed two hundred and eighty-one thoufand, four hundred and twelve fquare miles of territory ; a fpace equal to twice the area of the whole republic of France, which is known to comprehend *twenty-feven millions* of people. The writers on this fubject frequently remark, that large provinces of Hindoftan, were *formerly* cultivated like a garden. The Hindoos themfelves, are, perhaps, the moft abftemious of mankind. Their fubfiftence requires but a trifling quantity of food, compared with that of any race of people in Europe. From the pacific temper of the natives, they had, for the moft part, but few wars. Agriculture and manufactures had arrived at a high degree of perfection. From thefe important and combined caufes, the population of India muft have been prodigious. But, if we fuppofe that it was only in proportion to that of France, and the fuppofition is perfectly reafonable, the dominions of the Eaft-India company muft, before the commencement of Britifh conquefts, have contained *fifty-four millions* of inhabitants ; and from various circumftances that have been ftated, this computation is certainly not overcharged. For the fake of diftinctnefs, we fhall proceed by the help of cyphers.

Population previous to the year 1758 - - - 54,000,000
Lord Cornwallis, in 1789, ftates, that *one-third* part of this
   country, was, at that time, a jungle inhabited by wild
   beafts. For this jungle, deduct one-*third* of the ancient
   population - - - - - 18,000,000
Suppofe that the remaining two-third parts of thefe provinces have loft *only* one half of the thirty-fix millions of
   inhabitants, whom they contained, *before* their fubjection
   to the Britifh Eaft-India company. This one-half gives 18,000,000

Deduct this from the original population - - 36,000,000

Prefent number of inhabitants - - - - 18,000,000

Thus, in thirty-five years, that is, from 1758, to 1792, inclufive, there has been an uniform wafte of people, under thefe mercantile fovereigns, at the rate of more than *one million* per annum ; in whole, THIRTY-SIX MILLIONS. The premifes, on which this calculation has been founded, are explicitly placed before the reader. As to their juftice, he is competent to decide for himfelf.

THE END.

www.ingramcontent.com/pod-product-compliance
Lightning Source LLC
Chambersburg PA
CBHW030626270326
41927CB00007B/1331